THE PRIVATE LIFE OF THE ROMANOFFS

TRANSLATED FROM

THE GERMAN OF BERNHARD STERN

BY

SETH TRAILL.

The Romanoffs are reproached with having been tyrants. The truth is that these so-called autocrats of all the Russias have been nearly always slaves—slaves of their bejewelled mistresses and favorites.

Copyright © 2018 Read Books Ltd.
This book is copyright and may not be
reproduced or copied in any way without
the express permission of the publisher in writing

British Library Cataloguing-in-Publication Data
A catalogue record for this book is available from
the British Library

MANNERS, CUSTOMS AND DOMESTIC LIFE UNDER THE FIRST ROMANOFFS.

Russia's Misery.—Rescue by a Prince and a Serf.—Rise of the Romanoffs.—Michael Feodorovitsch, the first Romanoff Tzar.—The Patriarch Philaret Romanoff, the Bane of Russia.—Origin of the Romanoffs.—Commencement of the Romanoff Tyranny.—A Heretic Romanoff.—The Tzar Alexis Michaylovitch, the "Enlightened."—The Romanoff System of Favorites.—Tzarina and Doctor.—Marriage Customs of the Tzars.—Alexis Michaylovitch and Natalia Naryschkina.—Feodor Alexejevitch.—Ivan Alexejevitch, the Feeble.—Sophia Alexejevina, the Ambitious, and her favorite, Galitzin.—Peter Alexejevitch, the Great.—His Creations and Innovations.—Customs and Habits of His Epoch.—The Old and the New Times, a Masquerade.—A Wedding of Dwarfs.—Peter the Great and the Clergy.—The Papal Marriage.—Election of a New Pope by Besotted Cardinals.—Domestic Life in Old Russia.—Oriental Seclusion of Women.—Their Emancipation.—Ancient Marriage Ceremonies.—Enforced Marriages.—The Rod as a Dowry.—Assemblies.—Something About Drinking.—A Little Chapter on Immoralities.—A Comedy.

BLACK clouds overhung the Muscovite Empire after the terrible end of the terrible Ivan, after the fall of the false Dmitry. Tumult followed tumult. The cities fell into ruins, the villages became heaps of rubbish, fields and forests wasted into wildernesses. In the upper classes all was dissension, disloyalty and greed ; in the lower, slavish fear and fatalistic inactivity. Moscow fell into the hands of the Poles, who cruelly revelled and raged there. They destroyed the Kremlin-City of wood and stone, the churches and monasteries, profaned the health-bringing relics of the miracle workers, broke open the tombs of the saints and demolished their images. And when the patriarch dared to approach them with words of remonstrance, they dragged him off to prison and left him to perish miserably.

It was a mournful spectacle, and the Russian people longed for the day of their deliverance, longed for the hero who should bring order out of chaos and put an end to the strife.

At last a miracle was wrought. A Prince and a Serf, the Knjas Posharsky and the serf Kosma Minin, united for the rescue of Russia, incited the people to revolt and expelled the invaders. Then the two great Council Chambers assembled, the Bojar Chamber and Provincial Chamber, and the representatives of the whole Empire, Metropolitans, Archbishops, Bishops, Archimandrites and Igumes, Woywods, Bojars, Okolnitchy, Tschaschniky, Stolniky, Kossacks, Streltzi, Elders, Attamans, Gosty and Burghers—in short, "the best strongest and most intelligent of the people—" on February 21, 1613, chose Michael Fedorovitch to be their Tzar.

The Romanoffs were descendants of the Kambila, who migrated from Prussia and Lithuania in 1280, and soon gained a prominent position in the Russian Empire. Under Dmitry Donskoi, a Feodor Romanoff was Voyvod, and by the marriage of his daughter to the Prince of Tver, he became allied to the house of Rurik. Anastasia Romanovna, the first wife of Ivan the Terrible, was the mother of the Tzar Feodor, the last sovereign of the house of Rurik. Feodor Nikititsch Romanoff was the father of Michael, who was born the 12th of July 1596.

On the 19th of April, 1613, the old Kremlin-City, after her long sufferings, saw once more a happy day. Bright and beneficent was the spring-time sun that ushered in the first Romanoffs, bringing to the Empire the promise of peace and prosperity. The streets put on their gayest dress, the people shouted for joy. A few days before his entrance into the capital city the young Tzar had subscribed an act binding himself to protect religion, to hold the welfare of the people above all personal considerations, to leave the old laws unchanged and to make no new ones, to determine all weighty questions, not according to his own judgment, but by the laws of the land, to engage in no war and to conclude no peace without the consent of the Council Chambers, and for the avoidance of dissension, to transfer to other hands his private domains, or to make them over to the State as the property of the Crown.

Michael was by nature humane and benevolent, not devoid of magnanimity or unwilling to grant to the country and the people the liberty which was their right. He wished, rather, to reign as a constitutional sovereign, than which nothing better can be desired.

But, unhappily for Russia and for himself, he had a father—a father whose ambition knew no bounds. The latter, on becoming patriarch, had changed his burgher name of Feodor for that of Philaret. He soon succeeded in overshadowing his young son, the real Tzar. The patriarchate was as powerful as the throne. On nearly every document the name of Philaret appeared beside that of Michael. He not only took a share in all political matters, but put out ukases in his own name, to which as patriarch he had no title, and which even Michael would not have dared to do without the consent of the Council Chambers.

Philaret reigned in the Empire as absolutely as on his own domains, which he gradually enlarged and caused to be respected by the pious as church property, although they were in truth his own private benefices.

Thus arose the Romanoff despotism, the autocracy of the Tzars.

And the people, the good, unsuspecting people, knew nothing. The oaths which Michael had sworn on ascending the throne were forgotten; no one reminded him of them. Ere yet its loss was discovered the promised freedom was gone. The Romanoff era, so auspiciously begun, grew darker year by year. The laws had not brought to the people freedom and action, they had been transformed into shapeless knotty scourges, which subverted all free life, which stifled thought and feeling. Trade and intercourse were restricted; moral and physical distress were hermetically sealed up in a frozen silence.

And when Philaret at last, was no more, Michael continued to walk in the path which his father had pointed out. The Tzar who had ascended the throne with pledges to reign constitutionally, the liberal Tzar, was become an unbending autocrat. The Tzar is all, and all is his. Not only the people, not only the country. No, all products of the soil, all work of the hands, the air, the water and the light, are his.

Does the Tzar want workmen? He winks. And lo! out of all corners of the Empire, out of pathless space, out of the Asiatic wastes, from Siberian deserts, from the southern Steppes, from the fruit provinces of the West, they pour forth, slaves to work for their master, by day and night, and night and day, in winter and in summer, in the icy frost, under the burning sun, they come to work for him, unrequited. Unrequited, for the monarch pays no hire. Rejoice, wretched mortal that the great, the noble Tzar permits you to do and to suffer for him.

You are hungry, thirsty? You would fain rest after your toil? What is that to him? The poor commune may give you food and raiment, a place to sleep.

Trade is the monopoly of the Tzars. Earnings, also, are the monopoly of the Tzars.

No one must deal in any article until the Tzar has acquired his stock of the commodity on advantageous terms. Goods arriving from foreign countries must first be announced and offered to the crown. It has the right of purchase, it determines the price, or the goods that it will give in exchange. Only when it has been first satisfied may the " gosty " (merchants) be permitted to have what remains, which they are obliged to offer to the commercial houses of the Tzar, and before and above all things to care for his interests in preference to their own. Woe unto the man who is caught overreaching the throne!

Some there are, however, bold enough to engage in speculation, who even rise to a certain degree of affluence. But the prodigy is no sooner accomplished, a demamd for something is no sooner created, than an imperial ukase is issued establishing a monopoly for that article; the commodity is lowered in price, bought up and the value is then raised. All striving to rise is thus rendered futile, vain and useless all earnings, all acquisitions. The success of an industry in any place becomes its ruin. Immediately the imperial officials appear, and for weeks and months the hapless city must give its work unremunerated to the crown—must work until ruin comes upon it and the Tzar is forced to seek another place for his commissions. They are wisest, therefore, who live in idleness, or who content themselves with just so much labor as will enable them by a bare subsistence to win a reprieve from destiny.

Superstition holds the men of Russia enchained. There are no real schools; there are therefore almost no educated persons. Here and there are some who so call themselves, but in what does their education consist? For the most part in an acquaintance with psalms and prayers, in a little reading and writing.

Learning is pernicious; he who learns falls into heresy.

This statement is exact; experience has abundantly verified it.

Those are pronounced heretics into whose minds the desire of education has entered, those who have appropriated to themselves the "higher knowledge," who have had accursed thoughts, who have reflected on the strange condition of the country and asked themselves whether here all is as it should be.

There were some whom a strange freak of destiny at times permitted to glance beyond the boundary walls of Moscow, to learn something of foreign life, foreign customs and foreign freedom, and to compare the here and the there. Even the palace of the Tzar itself once sheltered such a freethinker, such a heretic.

This was Bojar Nikita Ivavowitch, the uncle of Tzar Michael.

He went (what audacity!) to a hunt in Polish costume. The patriarch burned with his own hand the heathen garb and required Nikita to purify himself with holy water. It might have been due to the mildness of this punishment that the heretic permitted himself practices more shameful still, for he had in his house (shocking to relate) a musical orchestra. All the threats of the Tzar and the curses of the priests availed nothing with this incorrigible freethinker. He procured a boat to be built for himself by heathen Dutchmen, and it was this boat which afterwards, found by Peter the Great, suggested to him the building of a Russian navy.

Tzar Michael died in 1645. His son, Alexis, then sixteen years old, succeeded him. Alexis Michaylovitsch is reported to have been an enlightened man. Let us look at his epoch, his reforms and the outcome of them. In the first years of his reign the warmest panegyrists of Alexis confess him to have been a canter and an idler, taking no interest in affairs of state, and leaving them in the hands of his favorite, Borofs Morosoff.

Morosoff was cunning and hard. The former tutor of the Tzar, he possessed his entire confidence, as to-day Pobedonofszef possesses that of Alexander the Third. Alexis went so far as to ally himself by marriage with his favorite. On the 16th of January, 1648, they married two sisters, the daughters of Elias Danilovitsch Miloslavsky. The favorite's arrogance now knew no bounds; he surrounded the throne with his relatives; he bled the people more than ever; they groaned, but their groans did not reach the ear of the Tzar. Heaven is high and the Tzar is far off—this was as true in the Russia of hundreds of years ago as it is in the Russia of to-day.

But the patience of the slaves was in the end exhausted. On the 26th of May, 1648, a bloodthirsty cry of revolution resounded through the streets of Moscow, and brutalized men and women rushed upon the palace of the imperial officials who were growing fat on the blood of the people. Moscow was surrendered to them to work their will, but the uproar did not cease. During long years it continued to rage in all quarters of the Empire. Wretchedness could not find means enough to satisfy itself with expiation. Alexis established a "council of secret officers" as a protection against the revolution. Siberia came into fashion as a place of banishment for political suspects, or criminals, and not without its effect.

It was now that Alexis discovered the mission which it was his to fulfil and set himself in good earnest to acquit himself of it. Of what is understood as reform he entertained no thought. He had no purpose to bring in anything new, but only to purify the old. In much he succeeded. Where he chiefly failed was in the eradication of bribery and drunkenness. Important acts of his which deserve recognition were the purification of the chambers of justice; an exact regulation of penalties, and the abolition of the death penalty for civil offenses.

To curb the arbitrariness of the officials, he ordained that every subject should be permitted free access to his person, and according to a pretty legend there was placed in front of his pleasure house at Kolomenskoje a tin box, a "mercy box," where every morning as he stepped to his window on rising, a crowd of petitioners was already gathered who under the eyes of their prince threw into it their grievances and requests.

Taxes were lightened, some of the privileges which discriminated in favor of the nobles against the poor were removed, commerce and intercourse were encouraged. The church texts were examined and amended.

The every-day history of Europe appeared to him of sufficient importance to induce him to have German newspapers now and then translated and distributed among the persons attached to his court. The Russians were, however, far from being curious to know promptly what was happening beyond their borders. It came to pass, therefore, that events which were already a year old were served up at the court of Moscow as burning news. The credentials of a Russian Ambassador to Spain in the year 1667, were addressed to King Philip IV, who had died two years before.

These acts won for Alexis the surname of "The Enlightened." But in the land of the enlightened Alexis, the treatment of woman was worse than in the whole remaining Orient. She was so completely secluded from all intercourse with the other sex that "The Enlightened" permitted a physician to visit the Tzarina only in a darkened chamber, and required him to feel her pulse through a silken stuff, the hand of a strange man not being suffered to touch hers. It was only in the closing years of his reign that relations were established which might be called easier.

The first wife of Alexis, the Tzarina Maria Iljinitschna, died, and in 1669 he brought a young wife into his palace at Moscow.

In former days, during the time of the prinpalities, the rulers chose their wives out of reigning Russian or foreign houses, especially those of Greece or Poland, once out of Polowzen Chanat. The Grand Dukes of Moscow followed the same practice until Wassily Ivanovitch first departed from it by taking a bride from among his subjects. His successors followed his example, as did also the first Romanoffs. When Alexis therefore decided to take another wife the Empire was ransacked, and seventy young girls of the greatest beauty were brought, from the abodes of the poor as well as from those of the rich, to the capital. The lord steward of the Tzar received the damsels and assigned to each her separate chamber in the imperial palace, where she was to reside until the period allotted for the choosing should expire.

All of the bride candidates ate at the same table, which permitted ample apportunity to make observations. Many a time Alexis attended them at the table disguised as a sleek waiter in order to study their deportment. But his presence did not remain a secret from the girls, nor did they ever forget to be well dressed and agreeable.

It was another thing when the Tzar undertook to make his observations by peering through the cracks and holes of their chambers. There his chances were better to study the behavior and mode of life of the damsels, each of whom was cherishing the hope of becoming the Tzarina of the Muscovite Empire.

As was natural, on all sides attempts were made to determine the Tzar in favor of this one or that. Meanwhile he had listened to the promptings of his own heart, and had chosen.

One day he summoned his principal steward and gave him this order:

"Let beautiful clothing be provided for sixty-nine of the young girls, and a bridal dress for the seventieth, whose name you shall know on the day of the choosing. Out of the marvellous wreath I have chosen a most precious flower. Nineteen times I have wandered through their apartments; for days and weeks I have observed the demeanor of each, and none of them surpasses her who is now the choice of my heart."

When on the morning of February 17, 1669, the domes of the Kremlin grew golden, the Lord Steward appeared with the bridal dress and asked to whom it was to be delivered. Alexis answered:

"Go to Natalia, the daughter of Kirill Naryschkin, and salute her as your Tzarina."

A few hours later the chosen one was solemnly united to Alexis. The remaining sixty-nine departed carrying rich presents to their houses or huts.

Natalia Kirillowna Naryschkina, who had suddenly become the Tzarina, was the daughter of a simple officer of dragoons and of a foreign woman named Hamilton.

In a former reign a Hamilton had come from Scotland to Russia, and his descendants had lived as servants of the crown in the German Sloboda, at Moscow. The Colonel of the regiment in which Kirill Naryschkin had served, whose name was Matwejef, had married a Hamilton, whose niece in her turn married a Naryschkin. Both he and Matwejef were of humble origin. To the Russians it was a simple matter of course that the Tzar should wed a low-born peasant girl, for "the Tzar needs neither riches nor a great family connection, but only a beautiful and virtuous spouse." But the marriage of the lowest Russian with the most exalted foreigner, a consort of the heathen-Roman, or the Lutheran faith, was in their eyes an abomination, and it mended matters but little for the bride to relinquish her faith for that of the orthodox church.

Matwejef and Naryschkin were viewed with scant favor by their fellows on account of these marriages, but they did not on that account repent of them; in fact Matwejef arrived at such a degree of prosperity that he was able to receive the daughter of Kirill into his house, where she was afforded the opportunity for a better rearing than was common in her time, for the house of Matwejef was unlike the houses of other Russians. The days of greater enlightenment which were about to dawn were casting there their first beams. European customs and manners prevailed, foreigners resorted there, the ambassadors from the various countries of Europe, and the so-called "enlightened minds" of the age. The women took part in the assemblages of the men, mingling with them in free, almost unrestrained intercourse. Thus Natalia Kirillovna had before her examples of manners and customs of which other Russian girls were in ignorance, and with the more graceful deportment thus acquired she easily ensnared the Tzar. And so it came about that the daughter of an apostate and of a foreign and heathen woman became Empress of Russia, and the mother of Peter the Great.

Her position was no easy one, but she really possessed the heart of the Tzar; so true and steadfast a spouse was he that she presumed to undertake the opening of a little, a very little street. After the death of Alexis, which took place in a few years, the entire charge of the education of young Peter fell to her; it was she who awakened in him a love of foreign customs, manners and culture; it was therefore she to whom Russia owed the extensive innovations which well-nigh transformed the Asiatic Empire into a semi-European country.

Alexis was succeeded in 1676 by his feeble son Feodor, at the age of fifteen. His early death in 1682 seemed to threaten Russia with a renewal of troublesome times. Feodor left no children, only an own and a half brother. The former, Ivan, the son of the first wife of Alexis, Maria Iljinitschna Miloslavska, was of full age but sickly and weak-minded; the other, Peter, was just ten years old. The energetic Natalia, his mother, succeeded in getting him called to share the throne with his brother Ivan, the rightful sovereign; she was not, however, able to prevent her step-daughter, Sophia, from being made regent instead of herself. With her favorite Galitzin, Sophia continued to hold the regency for seven years. But at length her rule came to an end.

Peter had lived in retirement. His great mind awoke and burst the fetters with which Sophia still sought to bind it. He quitted the town of Preobrashenskoje where he had been confined by his half sister, and suddenly appeared on the stage of the world. Young though he was, he showed that he possessed an indomitable will and great determination of character. Sophia was frightened, and employed members of the Strelitz bodyguard to murder him. But the young Tzar received warning of her intention, made his escape, and placing himself at the head of a body of soldiers of his own age who had hitherto been his playthings, he disposessed his ambitious sister and her favorite and seized the throne in his own name, deposing the feeble Ivan.

Scarcely had Peter grasped the reins of government than he set about the task of transforming the Empire,—of changing Asia into Europe, barbarism into civilization. Nothing should be permitted to remain which could recall men and days gone by, nor was anything too small or too insignificant to be new modelled after the European pattern, were the change for better or worse. And he wrought marvels. He made war, he founded a Russian navy, encouraged trade and commerce; he at least endeavored to check corruption and to foster education and learning. Yet remaining himself, in spite of all, rude and unpolished, he was ignorant of the correct methods to be employed to accomplish his designs. Education and civilization were placed under the protection of the knout; instead, therefore, of being heartily welcomed, they were tolerated, feared, and so far as possible, shunned. It was therefore a reform which extended no farther than the surface,—mere charlatanry. The country gained in power and consideration. It gained a culture and a civilization to which honest barbarism is far preferable. To the opinion that dress does not make the man, Peter opposed the conviction that a barbarian needs only to consent to change his garb to that of a European to become at once civilized; therefore the importance which he attached to the abolition of the old national dress in favor of the collar.

One day an Imperial mandate directed that all who drew pay from the Empire, and all possessing access to the court should appear in foreign dress. A pattern of such a costume was ordered to be displayed in front of every door in Moscow, St. Petersburg, and all large towns, and any one, not being a prince or a peasant, a Cossack, a Calmuck, or a Tartar—for these were as yet exempt—who passed through any gate clad in a long robe after the former fashion should pay a fine of two griefs, or twenty kopecks, or must kneel down and continue kneeling until so much of his robe as touched the ground was cut away.

The wearing of a long beard was incompatible with the new costume. As with Orientals the beard has been looked upon as a token of piety, so the Russians looked upon it as an attribute of the Christian faith, and to cut it off was to deface the image of God. How precious the beard was to the Russian appears from an ordinance of the Jaroslof code imposing a penalty fourteen times as great for a plucked out beard as for a cut off finger. That, however, gave Peter little concern; foreigners had smooth chins, therefore must Russians have them. The order was issued for the cutting off of beards, but permitting priests, peasants, and those who paid a tax of a hundred rubles to retain their beards. Even a peasant entering the city with his beard must pay a kopeck at the gate.

This measure soon brought the new costume into vogue in the capital, but to diffuse it throughout the distant quarters of the Empire was a less easy task. It happened often that over-zealous officials sought with Draconian severity to enforce obedience to the Tzar's command. In Woronesch, the city magistrates refused positively to conform to the order. At Easter the Tzar was to visit Woronesch, and Mentschikoff was anxious to prepare for his master a delightful surprise by procuring him a reception on the part of the magistrates with shaven chins. He ordered for them complete outfits of German apparel, and on Easter eve he sent for the magistrates and thus addressed them:

"I have received stringent orders from the Tzar to require you to wear these garments and to remove your beards. Will you obey? No? Then make yourselves ready for a journey to Siberia. The kibitks are in readiness to convey you thither."

The magistrates wept, implored, fell on their knees, protested that they would sooner lose their heads than their beards. Mentschikoff winked. Soldiers seized the men and were dragging them to their kibitks. The youngest of the number, who was but recently wedded, and who found the parting with his young wife even more grievous than the parting with his beard, exclaimed :

"I remain. Let the will of Heaven be done."

Mentschikoff winked again and a barber appeared and cut off the handsome beard of the young apostate.

This example will answer for many others. The shaving continued for a long time unpopular, and many pious Russians caused the beards of which they had been forcibly dispossessed to be restored to them in the grave.

The Raskolniky, or Old-Believers, persisted in refusing obedience to the new law. Peter did not care to combat too vigorously this powerful sect, he, therefore, permitted them to retain their beards in consideration of the payment of a stated fine or beard-tax. By way of a receipt and a certificate of their beard privilege they were given every year after the payment of the fine a coin called Borodowaja, or beard coin. On one side was a nose with a mustache and beard, on the other the inscription "paid tax" and the date.

To bring clearly before the eyes of his subjects the difference between the past and the present Peter ordered to be held on the occasion of the marriage of a court fool a ball according to the fashion of centuries gone by. The costumes to be worn should all be those of a hundred years ago. The Bojars came riding on strangely caparisoned horses, rudely attired and wearing prodigiously tall hats. Instead of a bridle, some of them held silver chains with links a finger and a half thick; the breasts and manes of their horses were bedecked with silver plates, making a jingling noise as they rode. The women, heavily veiled, arrived in uncomfortable two-wheeled Tatar carriages that tumbled and fell over every stone, while from the inside proceeded incessant screams and lamentations. Their dress was modelled after a long extinct fashion. Heavily ruffled sleeves fell down over their hands, and the heels of their shoes, ten inches high, had the appearance of stilts upon which the beauties swayed to and fro, with much difficulty preserving their center of gravity.

The festivities took place, like all those of the period, in the state palace of the Mentchikoffs.

Upon a throne with three steps, the pretended Tzar and Patriarch received the homage of the throng. Each guest was, on entering, saluted by his own and his father's name, and approaching reventially the Tzar and the Patriarch, kissed their hand and received as a gift of welcome a cup of brandy.

The feast was spread on a simple wooden table. The dishes, prepared in the manner of a time long past, disgusted palates grown accustomed to new receipts for cooking. Worse still was the brew concocted of meat and brandy which had been the favorite beverage of the olden time. Up to this time the guests had endured all without losing their equanimity; this was unendurable.

The repast over, the dancing began, and what a dance! In place of the graceful French and German dances to which the guests were accustomed, they saw jumping and stamping which filled them with amazement, and in which they could, with difficulty, execute their parts. And the music, the fearful music of the balayka, the gudoks and the bagpipe!

Lastly appeared the newly wedded pair. All were shivering with cold, there being, according to the old custom, no fire. A small bed made of rough boards beckoned to the bridal pair.

How they cursed the good old times!

Peter had a particular fancy for dwarfs. The court fool gave way to the dwarf, and he lost no opportunity to amuse himself with the little creatures.

On the occasion of the marriage of Prince Frederick William of Courland to the Russian Princess Anna, which took place the winter of 1710, he celebrated the nuptials of a pair of dwarfs with all the pomp that could have been observed at the marriage of a reigning prince. At this wedding the officials and attendants must be all of the same diminutive statures as the bridal pair. The whole empire was ransacked to procure seventy-two of the smallest specimens of humanity which it contained.

On the day before the wedding the two smallest of these little men were sent from house to house in a three-wheel miniature coach to invite the guests to the marriage; two other dwarfs rode on before on dwarf horses.

On the day of the ceremony Peter himself, according the custom of the Greek Church, held the wreath over the head of the bride.

The wedding festival took place in the Mentschikoff palace, in the same hall where two days previous the Tzar had received the guests who attended the wedding of the Princess Anna.

The dwarfs sat at a low table; the bridal party occupying two tables, were seated under silken canopies. The marshal and eight assistant marshals (also dwarfs) ran busily hither and thither. The Tzar and the gentlemen and ladies of the court sat as spectators on a bench along the wall. When the table was cleared they danced the Russian national dance, which the appearance of the dancers rendered very amusing. Some had tall backs and very short legs, some a huge belly, some wobbled on feet like an O, others on feet like an X; of some of them scarcely anything was to be seen but an enormously large head. Some had slanting mouths, some huge ears, and others, lastly, had tiny eyes and very thick lips. The gayeties were prolonged until near midnight, when the young pair were brought to the palace and assigned a residence.

The funeral of a dwarf was celebrated with the utmost pomp. Four priests in ecclesiastical garb, two of the Empress's marshals, and a choir of thirty singers walked in front of the corpse. A sleigh drawn by six small horses conveyed the coffin covered with black velvet, and in it also rode the surviving brother of the dwarf, a dwarf fifty years old. Immediately behind came the other mourners—twelve pairs of dwarfs dressed in black, wearing long cloaks and crape, were followed by twelve pairs of female dwarfs ranged in order according to their sizes, while the Tzar, his ministers, generals and officials, closed the cortege.

These innovations brought the Tzar, for the most part, but little sympathy. He soon came to be regarded as an apostate, and there were not wanting those who applied to him the epithet of Satan, especially by reason of his infringement upon the rights of the clergy, and his presuming to abolish the dignity of patriarch and in its place to create a body dependent upon the Tzar, the Holy Synod.

He ended at last by leaving nothing to the priests. One Sunday the Tzar appeared as the Summus Pontifex, and in a loud voice conducted the prayers and the preaching. A contemporary * observes of him : " He is a God-fearing and warlike Joshua, who not only lifts up his hands in prayer but employs them for the government and defence of his people—

---

* Des grossen Herrn Czaars and Grossfursten von Moskau Petri Alexowicz Leben und Thaten. Franckfurt, 1710.

with what reverence, by his diligent attendance at church does he not call upon God for the welfare of his country, and would have His holy word reverenced in all hearts to bring blessings to his subjects."

To the ecclesiastics this was naturally an abomination, and a great crying and lamentation went up over the "Satan Tzar." Peter therefore, seeking for a means of ruining the clergy determined to make them ridiculous. He made a pope of his former tutor, Sotof, now an old man of eighty-four, feeble in mind, and married him to a pretty young widow. A great feast was prepared in honor of the singular nuptials, in which fourteen hundred persons, men and women, Bojars and peasants, with their families, took part. The four persons who, according to Russian usage, deliver the invitations a few days before the wedding, were the greatest stutterers that could be found in the Russian Empire. For marshals, best men, and masters of ceremony, decrepit old men were chosen, for runners thick-bodied gouty persons. A Bojar represented the Emperor on the occasion, dressed to represent King David, but instead of a harp he held a lyre which was enwrapped with the skin of a lion and which he turned around and around.

The procession passed through all the streets of St. Petersburg. The sham Tzar was seated in a large sleigh on a high scaffolding with enormous bears at either end, which from time to time were made to growl horribly by being stuck with sharp instruments. Peter himself wore the guise of a Friesland peasant, and he, with three others similarly disguised, beat upon drums. The remainder of the guests were ranged in fours with different costumes and instruments. Amid the ringing of all the bells in the capital the procession arrived at the cathedral. The ill-assorted pair proceeded to the altar and were united in marriage by a priest a hundred years old. Two lights were held up before his bespectacled nose, while some one shouted into his ear what he should say. From the church they proceeded to the palace of the Tzar, where the sport degenerated into a Bacchic carousal.

One day the sham Pope died. They proceded to the election of his successor with solemn ceremonial. The election was arranged to take place in the house of the deceased Pope, in which were placed two huge wooden bells and sixty-four stone ones, all of which were rung at once and gave forth a terrible din. In the electoral chamber, the walls of which were hung with straw matting, a throne was set up six steps high, covered with red linen, and in the centre of it was a barrel of beer painted red and blue, and upon this sat a living Bacchus, namely, a man who for eight days had not been permitted to become sober. At the right of the throne was a seat for the sham Tzar, and on the left, one for the Pope who was to be elected. Along the wall stood thirteen perforated chairs for the cardinals. The adjoining room, the "conclave chamber," was separated into fourteen boxes by straw matting. In each box instead of a light hung a wooden shoe, and in the middle were a bear and ass made of clay, with barrels of brandy near by.

All the cathedral bells rang out as the strange procession began its march. At its head stalked a marshal in his usual dress and carrying a red staff. Next to him came twelve pipers representing the Pope's pages, who carried spoons with little bells, and these were followed by the chief functionaries and officers, Ministers, Generals, Ambassadors, priests, real and false, the Emperor, a dwarf as secretary of the pope, and six stutterers as the Pope's heralds. Upon a barrel of brandy borne by sixteen drunken peasants, collected from the tap-houses, sat a drunken fellow as Bacchus. Before this reeling barrel staggered a feeble old man brandishing to and fro a burning pine branch, which represented incense. Another barrel of brandy and another Bacchus were borne by twelve bald-heads, who carried hog-bladders in their hands. The cardinals brought up the train pressing to their hearts books which looked like prayer-books, but which contained only songs in praise of Bacchus.

When the procession reached the fore-court of the electoral house it was greeted with cheers of welcome and the beating upon empty barrels by wooden hammers. While the remainder of the company assembled in the different rooms, drinking and merry-making, the cardinals were shut up in the conclave chamber where they were to remain all night. In addition to their usual drinking they were required to swallow every quarter of an hour an enormous spoonful of brandy. In the morning the besotted conclave was liberated to announce its choice, upon which however it was no easy matter to agree. There was no one of them but would gladly have been invested with the mock dignity, for it carried with it an annual stipend of a thousand rubles. In addition to this the pretended Pope was presented with a residence in St. Petersburg and in Moscow, and was at liberty to draw upon the Imperial cellars for all the wine, brandy and beer he might desire, or which his household could use. Lastly, every one, high or low, was required to observe toward him the same respect as if he had been the real *Summus pontifex*, under penalty of a heavy fine.

It will readily be seen, therefore, that the cardinals could not promptly agree. A word from the Tzar was needed to decide them, and the choice fell upon the commissary Strogost. He was placed upon the throne. All approached him and kissed his slipper, while he, puffed up with pride in his chimerical pontificial dignity, offered each a spoonful of brandy. He was then placed breast high in a barrel of brandy out of which he offered to all a drink. Lastly the feast was served. The real Abbess Galitzyn and three nuns served the viands which consisted of skilfully prepared cats, mice, foxes, bears, wolves, and other similar animals. They drank bravely withal until a late hour of the night. Then they separated, promising that on the next occasion they would crown the Pope.

The next occasion which brought them all

again together was the funeral obsequies of the Tzar.

In the matter of innovations the women were in better accord and yielded the Tzar a more willing obedience than the men, for women love changes of fashion. Furthermore they received, together with the foreign dress, certain other advantages.

Up to this time they had been kept in strict confinement, seldom venturing elsewhere than to the baths, the churches and cloisters, and to the houses of their relatives, and this only when closely veiled or in well closed carriages or sleighs. Even in the weddings in their own houses they did not show themselves in the presence of strangers. On special occasions only, where the master of the house desired to show marked honor to his guest, he called to the table his wife and daughter, who kissed the stranger, and after presenting him a little cup of gin immediately made the *poklon*, or adieu, and departed.

Those whose rigorous lords possessed sufficient means, kept dwarfs who entertained their mistresses with jokes, told them tales, and whose office it was besides to stimulate their senses by gently rubbing their heads or tickling their feet. The poor women, given over to drunkenness and idleness, could be seen lying for weeks on the ovens, eating, drinking and sleeping. Suddenly all this was changed. Scarcely had Peter ascended the throne than he dashed in pieces the oppressive fetters with which the women had been burdened. He issued orders that the dress of the women of Russia should conform to the fashion of that worn by foreign women, and introduced for them gowns of German, French, English and Dutch patterns. The question of fashion in dress then held an important place in the history of the world. The women who dressed according to the new fashions were free, those who wore the old costumes were immured. That they needed not to be long entreated to adopt the former garb need not be said—and above all, since in the new costume they gained admission to the entertainments of the court. New paths opened up to those who had until now been slaves and they obeyed for the most part with joy the Tzar's behests. The men were not all so well pleased, and many a woman dreading the wrath of her orthodox spouse, dared not follow her desires, and attended the ball by the Tzar's order accompanied by the police.

Another innovation of the Tzar's which has

a historical interest was the abolition of enforced marriages. The destiny of children was entirely in the hands of their parents. When a daughter was grown up, her parents proposed to some unmarried man to offer her to his parents, praising the charms of the fair one with all the energy of the vender of a quack article. If an understanding was arrived at between the parents, the wedding took place without delay, and before the bridal pair had seen each other. The bridegroom with his friends and the priest walked in procession to the home of the bride, who in the presence of her companions received him with a kiss and offered him a cup of gin in token of her consent. Then she covered herself with her veil and continued veiled until the ceremony was ended.

After the exchange of a ring by the parents of the bridal pair, the bridegroom proceeded to the church followed by the bride in a covered carriage or sleigh drawn by a horse completely covered with fox tails. After the ceremony the priest presented the newly wedded pair with a large glass of gin, which, after they had drunk to his health, he threw on the ground and the bride stamped on it, saying: "So may be dashed in pieces whatever may presume to create discord and enmity between man and wife."

Then the bride's father stepped up to her, and holding up a pine rod struck her with it saying : "This, my dear daughter, is the last blow you will receive from my hand. I release you from the parental authority and deliver you into the hands of your husband. If you should fail to show him the obedience which is his due, with this rod he will remind you of your fault."

With these words the father delivered to his daughter the little pine branch which, to the orthodox Russian, was an object of as great respect as the wedding ring.

After these pretty preliminaries the bride was led to the bridegroom's house.

How could a union so contracted prosper? Not only no affection could spring up between the husband and wife, but the subjection of the wife was so complete that she could not but hate her tyrant. For his ill treatment she revenged herself when she could with unfaithfulness, while he in his turn avenged his wrongs with cruel punishments, even with death.

Peter wished to alleviate the wretchedness of the women, and he regarded as the first step to that end the abolition of enforced marriages.

He ordained that no marriage should take place without the free will and consent of the parties, who should be permitted to see each other for the space of at least six weeks previous to the wedding.

The Russian women of that day, according to the unanimous testimony of contemporary travellers, were very pretty. According to their own standard no one was pretty who had not a very red complexion. When the Russians wished to describe a beautiful women, they said her face is very red. And if nature had not favored them with this ornament they did not fail to procure it by means of art, thus they painted themselves insufferably. The peasant girl on the roadside, the beggar girl in the city, did not ask for bread but for a couple of kopecks to buy paint. Stoutness of form was also an enviable gift; black teeth were much in vogue, and beauty plasters in all sorts of figures—flowers, trees, carriages, horses or other animals.

The girls generally wore their hair in two braids down their backs fastened at the ends with large gay tassels. The married women wore their's concealed under a cap.*

---

* The peasant women were less eager than those of the city to conform to the new fashions. They remained at home and adhered for the most part to the old order and

Women of the higher ranks dressed according to Peter's order, in foreign fashions. Yet it happened that many were at a loss how to accommodate themselves to the strange costumes, and a distinguished Russian dame might be met splendidly attired in the French or German fashion, in silk and satin, bedecked with laces and ribbons, barefooted, and carrying her slippers in her hands, being ignorant for what purpose they were intended.

In order to promote sociability among the officials of his court and the residents of the capital and to bring about easy intercourse between men and women, Peter instituted entertainments to which he gave the name of Assemblies, and the busy Tzar found time to compose and draw up himself the rules for the conduct of these Assemblies:

---

disorder, continued to go barefooted and to wear rough shoes like the men. In the summer they wore only a long thin blue linen sleeveless smock fastened with a girdle and which they seldom removed; in winter over the smock they wore a sheepskin. On their neck they wore a string of glass pearls, and earrings with three pendants one below the other. Lastly, on their breast they wore a leaden cross, which was never removed except when about to engage in some excess. These little crosses were worn by the men also. They were so sacred and so indispensable to a Russian that few were buried without them.

ORDINANCE FOR THE HOLDING OF ASSEMBLIES IN ST. PETERSBURG.

1. Assembly is a French word which it is not easy to express in Russian. It means a number of men who, for amusement or to converse on more serious matters, have met together. Friends upon meeting each other may converse together, can learn news of each other, and inform themselves of the events which are happening in the world.

2. The order to hold assemblies applies to every prominent person of the Court about once every winter, and the Chief of Police will give notice to him at whose house it shall be the pleasure of the Tzar that an assembly shall take place.

3. The person at whose house the assembly is taking place has been required to place a notice thereof in front of his house and to give information of it to all, both men and women.

4. The assembly shall not begin before four or five o'clock of the afternoon or continue later than ten of the evening.

5. The host is not required to receive or to attend upon the guests, or to constrain them to eat and drink. He is, however, required to furnish chairs, lights, drinks and diversions.

6. No person is required to come or to go at a certain hour; it is enough that he has let himself be seen at the assembly.

7. Every one shall be free at an assembly to sit, to walk, or to play, and no one shall be permitted under pain of the great eagle, that is to say, of the emptying of the great goblet, to reproach him therewith.

8. Persons coming to an assembly are required to salute only upon entering and departing.

9. No one shall be presented with more wine or brandy to drink than he wishes.

10. Whoever violates the laws of the assemblies or offends against good behavior shall be punished with a heavy portion to drink.

11. Persons of rank, such as nobles, and officers of high grade, also well-known merchants and shipbuilders, households of Chancellors, together with the wives and children of the same, may attend the assemblies without further notice.

12. Lackeys, excepting those belonging to the host's household, shall have a space assigned to them, in order that there shall be plenty of room.

That the assemblies were merry enough, is

clear. The drinking was terrible. Drunkenness was so common in the Russia of Peter's time that it was scarcely held to be a vice. Some travellers assure us that the Russians of that day were very much inclined to regard it as a part of religion, and thought that they had not fittingly celebrated a feast day if they had not been intoxicated the night before.

A strange custom was that which prevailed in even the most refined circles of forcibly compelling the guests to drink by closing the door and stationing sentinels before it to prevent any one from leaving without his allotted cargo.

Peter, on one occasion, gave an entertainment in honor or a German ambassador at his palace of Peterhof. At dinner the guests were plied with Tokay until none of them could stand on their feet, nevertheless each of them must accept from the soft hand of the Tzarina a quart of brandy, which completely finished him. The Tzar alone had the prudence to abstain, and could, therefore, find his amusement in the befuddled condition of his guests. He caused them to be carried off, some into the garden, some into the woods, and others into different apartments. At four o'clock they were carried into a forest where the Tzar set them to work to fell a row of trees, himself setting the example. After a few hour's work they had sweated away the fumes of wine. At supper they received as their reward another heavy cargo and went to bed senseless. At eight o'clock in the morning they were invited to coffee which consisted of a large cup of brandy. After this they were set upon rough cart horses to ride up a steep hill and around and about a forest. At dinner they were treated to a fourth bout and immediately after took ship with the Tzar to Kronschlott in a heavy storm, where they ran the risk of their lives.

There were also theatrical performances as well as Assemblies. The sister of Peter, the Princess Natalia, wrote the plays in Russian, gathering her material partly from the Bible, partly from secular chronicles. Actors (and musicians) were Russian. The wag, an officer, intermixed the play with jests of his own which had no manner of connection therewith. Lastly, an orator appeared and delivered a lecture of admonitions to the audience.

The abrupt transitions which Peter had effected were not slow in showing the evil of their workings, and the sudden and unwonted freedom of intercourse between men and women, which should have served to moderate the rudeness and drunkenness of the men, was the occasion of an immorality which knew no bounds.

The women did not know how to understand their freedom. They looked upon immodesty and indecent behavior as the expressions of it. The more shameless they could be, the greater the advance they had made in the direction of freedom and emancipation. A contemporary traveller groans over the immorality of the Russian women, and says: "The women are shameless and wanton. It is nothing strange in Russia to see the women strip themselves publicly for the bath and come out of it naked. Forty, fifty and more Russian women and girls dance and jump about in a state of nature without being in the least abashed by a passing stranger."

Peter himself set his people the worst example of immorality, which was reason enough why he should visit others with severe punishment on account of it. In his Army Regulations the following interesting paragraph appears:

CHAPTER III, WHICH RELATES TO IMMORALITY.

Art. I.

A prostitute shall not be suffered in garrison, or on a march, or in camp, but shall be immediately denounced and cast out.

Art. II.

As indecent language leads to unchastity, it, as well as lewd songs, is forbidden under heavy penalties.

Art. III.

Adultery will be punished according to the laws of the State to which the offender belongs.

Art. IV.

Rape will be punished with death.

Art. V.

Unnatural crime will be punished with burning.

That the Tzar was capable of treating such serious matters with humor is shown by the following incident which took place in Moscow in 1724, and caused much amusement:

An eminent Russian who was well advanced in years was married to a young and pretty wife who had a lover. One day the wife and her paramour were surprised by the sudden apparition of the husband upon the scene. The gallant in his embarrassment and haste seized the husband's trousers in place of his own, which contained his gold watch, a heavy gold purse, and other valuables. When the injured husband discovered the booty, he came to the rational conclusion that for the sake of the precious trousers he would swallow in silence his grievance and disgrace. Not so well contented was the beloved fugitive. The loss of his trousers afflicted him so sensibly that he determined to make an effort to recover them. With this view he approached the old man as he was leaving the church, drew him aside, kissed his hands and his feet, implored forgiveness for his offense and begged to have his trousers returned to him. The wily old husband upbraided him for his foolish talking, which he declared resembled the ravings of a madman, praised his wife as a pattern of virtue and conjugal fidelity, and departed, leaving the young man annihilated. He then went and threw himself at the feet of the Tzar, confessed his fault and begged for his assistance.

But the Tzar pronounced this judgment : " To the husband belongs all that he shall find upon the marriage bed." *

---

*Sigismund Herberstein, Commentarius rerum Moscoviticarum, Antv. 1557. Ant. Possevini, Moscovia, Colon, 1587. Neugebauer, Historical Russiæ, Moscovia, 1612. Petri Petreji, Moscowitische Chronica, Leipzig, 1620. Samuel Collins, The Present State of Russia, London, 1667. A Relation of Three Ambassadors from His Sacred Majesty Charles the Second to the Great Duke of Moscov, etc., by Carl Carlis, London, 1668. Nicholas Witsen, Travels in Russia and Tartary, Amsterdam, 1671. Reutenfels De Rebus Moscoviticis, Patav, 1680. Alberti Heidenfeld, Beschreibung der Orientalischen Konigreiche Turckey, Perse in, Moscau und China, Franckfurt, 1680. Daniel Prinz a Buchau, Moscovici ortus et Progressus, de Ducibus Moscoviæ, etc., 1680. Prinz Buchau, De Rebus Moscoviticis, Patav, 1680. Histoire de Moscovie par Meyerberg. L'Etat du Grand Duc de Moscovie, Paris, 1680. Das grossed und Machtige Reich Moskowien, Nurnberg, 1687. Aegidius Fletcher, De Rebus Russicis. Tauneri Legatio in Moscoviam, Norimb., 1689. Georg Adam Schleusings Neuentdecktes Sybirien, Jena, 1690. Adam Olearius, Moscowitische und Persianische Reyssbeschreibung, Hamburg, 1696. Allison, Voyage from Archangel in Russia in the Year 1697. Histoire Curieuse de Moscovie. A la Haye, 1699. Der Moscowitische Statt., 1702. Kurze Beschreibung von Moscowien, Nurnberg, 1711. Treuers Einleitung zur Moscow. Historie, Leipzig, 1720. Salmon, Der Staat von Russland, Altona, 1742. Strahlenberg, Northern and Eastern Europe, Stockholm, 1750. Schiemann, Russland bis ins Siebzehnte Jahrhundert, Berlin, 1884. Bruckner, The Question of Women in Russia in the Time of Peter the Great. Russian Review,

XV., 120. Kleinschmidt, Russlands Geschichte, Dargestellt in der Seines Adels, Cassel, 1877. Bruckner, Bilder aus Russlands Vergangenheit, Leipzig, 1887. W. Pierson, Aus Russlands Vergangenheit, Leipzig, 1870. Bruckner, Die Europaisierung Russlands, Gotha, 1880. Engelmann, Peter the Great, an Exposition, Dorpat, 1872. De la Marche, Anecdotes Russes, Londres, 1764. Crusenstolpe, Der Russische Hof., Hamburg, 1855, Vol. 1. Hermann, Geschichte des Russischen Staates, Leipzig. Rambaud, Histoire de la Russie, Paris, 1878. Hupels nordische und Neue nordische Miscellanen, Riga, 1782, 19 Bande. Ustrjalows History of Russia. Galitzin, La Russie au XVIII. siecle, Paris, 1863. Schlosser, Geschichte des 17, und 18. Jahrhunderts. Ssolowjew, History of Russia.

MARRIAGE AND AMOURS OF PETER THE GREAT.

Peter's Early Excesses.—His Marriage with Eudoxia Lopuchina.—Difference of Character.—Eudoxia's Hatred of Mentschikoff.—The Favorite's Revenge.—Eudoxia's Banishment.--Her Supposed Love Affair.—Her Revenge on Mentschikoff.—The Noble Anna Mons.—Peter's Mistresses.

THE difficulties and dangers in which Peter's youth had been passed had hardened and embittered him, so that while his mind soared to the highest spheres of thought and knowledge, his soul was stained by the basest passions. While yet a boy, in the company of his wild associates he gave himself up to dissipation and profligacy, while his mother passed her days in bitterness and her nights in anxiety.

When he reached the age of sixteen, Natalia Kirillovna determined to choose for him a wife, hoping thus to bring him to lead a more quiet and regular existence. She called upon the Bojars and Vovwods of the Empire to send their daughters to Moscow. This was the last time that a Russian ruler followed the old custom of choosing a wife from among the daughters of the land.

The summons was obeyed and the Vovwods and Bojars sent their daughters, those of them at least who were comely and graceful, to Moscow. The choice of the Tzarina after observing the damsels fell upon Eudoxia Feodorovna, the daughter of Feodor Abramovitch Lopuchin, a prominent and wealthy noble. On the 27th of January, 1689, the wedding was celebrated with pomp, and Eudoxia ascended the throne which she was to share with Peter Alexejevitch.

It is certain that Eudoxia loved her husband and was for a moment at least loved by him for her beauty, but she was not able long to enchain the Tzar. She was without education, as her letters show, and had no interest in the affairs that actively engaged Peter. To the Tzar's restless activity she opposed a cold indifference. She lived like an oriental, never showing herself in public, driving in a well closed and curtained carriage, and in the early morning or late evening, that she might not be seen by any one. Her carriage was lined with red velvet and drawn by six horses. On either side rode a numerous train of attendants in full dress military uniform. She had her chapel in the palace where she and her ladies worshipped, and never attended a public place of worship.

To Peter, on the other hand, the restricted life of his forefathers was irksome. He wished to be seen every day by his subjects, and to mingle with them without restraint. Associating with foreigners, especially, was his delight.

The Tzarina was peevish and faultfinding, and greeted the Tzar upon his return from amusements in which light women took part, with long curtain lectures, which to the autocrat of all the Russias could not but be insupportable.

In addition to all this, Mentschikoff, the Tzar's all-powerful favorite, hated his master's wife and neglected no opportunity to irritate him against her. Eudoxia had accused him in the presence of ladies and gentlemen of the Court of corrupting and misleading the Tzar, and of enticing him into the society of loose women who had patronized him when he was selling cakes. This taunt Mentschikoff never forgave. He vowed vengeance, and the favorite triumphed over the wife.

One night, returning late from one of his revels, on being reproached by Eudoxia for his drunkenness and profligacy, the Tzar was roused to such a pitch of fury that she was forced to fly from him in terror. From this time the breach was complete, although Peter did not go so far as openly to repudiate his wife during the lifetime of his mother. But on January 25, 1694, Natalia Kirillovna died, and with her all that the Tzar had held in respect. He forthwith gave notice to Eudoxia that she was to retire to a convent for the remainder of her life. And she was then just twenty.

She refused to obey. Then Mentschikoff came to the help of his master. He proved to his satisfaction that Eudoxia had been implicated in the revolt of the Streltzi, as a punishment for which she was divested of everything she possessed and banished to the convent of Ssushdal where she lived many years as Sister Helena. But her troubles did not end here. When, years after, her son Alexis was brought to trial, Mentschikoff appeared as her accuser. It was charged that in the offices of a church adjoining the convent, Eudoxia was recognized as the Tzarina; that she had worn the garb of a nun for a brief space only ; that she had maintained a correspondence with a Major Gljeboff, and had been implicated with him in intrigues against the Tzar.

The first three charges were true; she was found guilty also of the fourth. In Eudoxia's letters to Gljeboff however there is no reference to politics, but only to love. They are filled with expressions of the most ardent passion, and bear witness to depth and warmth of feeling, to a nature in which there was love enough to forgive. In contrasting her cold conventional letters to Peter with the ardent passion of her letters to Gljeboff, one must regret that the Tzar had not won her heart for himself. Once and only once, and as if by constraint, does an endearing expression for the Tzar escape her pen.

The discovery of the relations between the deposed Tzarina and Major Gljeboff infuriated Peter. He is said to have applied with his own hand the torture and knout to force from her a confession of guilt. Gljeboff, also, was put to the torture, but he maintained to the last Eudoxia's innocence. As a punishment for his "obduracy" he was impaled alive, and it was several hours before death, which found him in full possession of his senses, came to end his sufferings. The Tzar was present and witnessed his martyrdom. When Gljeboff saw him he spat in his face, exclaiming: "Go! Tyrant! Let me at least die in peace."

Eudoxia was confined like a common offender in the convent of Staraja Ladoga, at Schlüsselberg, where she lived on bread, water and greens, until her grandson Peter ascended the throne. She was then recalled to the court, and came with joy to assist in the fall of her mortal enemy, Mentschikoff. His banishment to Siberia was due to her efforts in a great measure. Her work of vengeance accomplished, she withdrew again into obscurity, and lived in retirement until her death on the 10th of September, 1731.

After his separation from Eudoxia Peter abandoned himself to a life of profligacy. The great ruler who had lifted the Empire out of barbarism remained himself a barbarian, incapable of imposing upon himself the slightest restraint. He who punished with cruel severity the least transgression on the part of his subjects, went himself from crime to crime. Womanhood had no sacredness for him. After Prince Wladimir of Kiev, he must have been the one of all the Russian rulers who perverted the largest number of women.

The morals of the court of Peter were of the worst description, and only one young and beautiful woman is said to have resisted his wooing. The memory of these women, who participated in many affairs of State and to whose laxity of morals many illustrious houses owe their origin, has for the most part passed away. A few names only have been preserved as associated with the loves of Peter.

Anna Mons de la Croix, according to some a Livonian and the daughter of an innkeeper, according to others the descendant of a noble and distinguished Dutch house, was the one woman of Peter's court who disdained the Tzar's rough wooing. All agree in describing her as a model of perfect womanhood. To the most fascinating beauty she united a pure and noble character, sensibility without sentimentalism, a waywardness which piqued without becoming wilfulness, a vivacity which did not contradict the goodness of her heart, and a playful wit which attempered the circumspection of her behavior. These qualities which won her an ascendency in the circle in which she moved, could not fail to attract the notice of the Tzar. He offered her his love bluntly and concisely, and she as bluntly and concisely repulsed him.

Peter renewed his suit almost humbly, accompanying it with the most tempting offers, and with a present of a house in St. Petersburg. But Anna Mons remained insensible, and quietly and gravely repelled him. The enamoured Tzar, his passion increasing with the resistance it encountered, was resolved to stop at nothing to accomplish his purpose. He was ready even to marry Anna Mons and to make her Empress, if she was not otherwise to be won.

But Anna secretly loved another—Baron Kaiserling, the German ambassador at St. Petersburg. Mentschikoff, dreading the loss of his own influence through the Tzar's love for Anna Mons, slipped into the latter's hands one evening upon his arrival late at a ball, a letter in which Anna complained to her betrothed of the Tzar's persecutions. This discovery changed Peter's love into rage and hate. After a stormy scene he was ungenerous enough to demand the restoration of the house with which he had presented her.

Anna left the ball in haste, and informed her betrothed of what had happened. Kaiserling now resolved to marry her at once and protect her from a fresh outburst of the Tzar's wrath. But he suddenly and unaccountably sickened and died, and the marriage took place on his deathbed. After the death of her husband

Anna's life was rendered inexpressibly painful by the persecutions of the greatest of Russian rulers until his death twenty years later.*

Peter had not similar obstacles to encounter in storming the heart of a sister of Anna's, the wife of General Balk. Although a woman well advanced in years, she long held the Tzar a captive. She played no very important role, however, as his mistress, but came after his death to be much talked of in connection with the tragic love affair of her brother.

The shining role in connection with the amours of Peter the Great was played by the daughter of a serf, afterwards Catharine I. The history of the world has not another woman whose destiny can be compared with hers. Born a serf, she became successively the wife of a soldier, the mistress of two Russian generals, the mistress and then the wife of the greatest of Russian monarchs, and herself the ruler of the greatest empire in the world. And at her death after a reign of two years the

---

*Bruckner has several times asserted that Peter had "relations" with Anna for ten years. These relations were not, however, very intimate. That Peter desired Anna to become his mistress is certain. But it is no less certain that she resisted him. Bruckner asserts also that she married the Prussian Ambassador Kaiserling and soon after died. That is an error.

courts of Europe wore mourning for her during many weeks.

Peter was guilty of a very base action toward a young woman of Hamburg. While on a visit to that city in 1716—in the company of Catharine, be it remarked—he made the acquaintance of the daughter of a Lutheran clergyman. To see her and to be enamoured of her were one and the same thing. She was not herself averse to becoming the passing plaything of the Tzar, but her father refused positively to sacrifice his daughter to the imperial profligate. He demanded that Peter should leave the girl in peace, or discard Catharine and marry her in due form.

Peter accepted the latter alternative, the documents were drawn up, and the ceremony performed. The next morning, however, he returned the minister his daughter and demanded the return of the marriage contract.

A noteworthy mistress of Peter's was Anna Ivanovna Kramer, the beautiful daughter of a merchant of Narva. After the capture of that city by the Russians she was brought to Kasan on the Upper Volga, passed into the hands of General Balk at St. Petersburg, and by him was presented to Miss Hamilton, a maid of honor, as her waiting maid. In this way the Tzar saw her, and the sprightly damsel who be it said had many a tender recollection behind her, attracted his attention and awakened his interest. He became a frequent visitor at the house of Miss Hamilton. During these visits Miss Kramer had to be admitted to the family circle, and she understood how to employ the arts of coquetry so as to captivate the Tzar. To be able to see her more frequently he gave her a position in the palace, and she preserved for a long time his favor and confidence. She was one of the few who were in the secret of the murder of the Tzarevitch. After General Weide had cut off the Prince's head, the Emperor invited his mistress into the apartment where lay the headless corpse, and she sewed the head to the body while still dripping with blood and dressed it for exhibition in the church.

Soon after this ghastly deed Anna Ivanova yielded her place to others, but the Tzar did not forget her service to him of which with surprising steadfastness not a word escaped her, and rewarded her richly with money and lands. After the death of Peter she returned to Narva where she lived a half century longer, dying in 1770 at the age of seventy-six.

The Miss Hamilton, who has already been

mentioned, was another of the Tzar's mistresses, and bore him a child. As Peter's amours were short-lived Miss Hamilton was soon discarded. She reproached him bitterly, but her reproaches being without effect, by way of revenge she murdered the child to whom Peter was very much attached. She paid for her vengeance with her life. The Tzar caused her to be beheaded, and presented her head to the Academy of Sciences with instructions to preserve it carefully. The head of the woman soon had as its companion the handsome head of a man.

These were passing caprices which Catharine might view with tolerable indifference. A more serious affair was his fancy for the young Princess Kantemir, which in the latter years of his life came to possess much significance.

The Kantemir family were reputed to be descended from Chan Timur, the Asiatic world-stormer. Dmitry, a son of the Moldavian Woyvod Constantine Kantemir, came to St. Petersburg in 1711, was raised to the rank of prince and became a favorite of Peter the Great. He was a zealous friend of the Academy of Sciences, and wrote a *historia de ortu et defectione imperi turcici*. His son, Antioch Dmitryjevitch, was the first Russian satirist, and his daughter—the last of Peter's mistresses.

The Princess Kantemir was reputed one of the most beautiful women of her time, and Peter was so much enamoured of her as to be willing for her sake to repudiate Catharine. Their relations grew still closer when there was the promise of the birth of a child, perhaps a son, for whom the Emperor ardently longed. But the birth was premature, and angered by the disappointment Peter broke off with her and returned to Catharine, who regained so completely her old ascendency that the Tzar crowned her and named her his successor. Scarcely had he done this than her scandalous relations with the Chamberlain Mons came to light.

Peter's vengeance was terrible, and the doom of Catharine appeared to be sealed. At this stormy period the Princess Kantemir reappeared at court, and the Tzar, seeing himself betrayed turned again to her. He discovered that the miscarriage of the Princess had been brought about by Doctor Policula, Catharine's tool, and formed the design to repudiate her and raise the Princess to the throne.

But swifter than the vengeance of the Tzar was the sickle of death. It cut off Peter the Great before he had accomplished his design.

Des grossen Herrens Czaars Petri Alexowiz Leben und Thaten. Ton J. H. von L. Franckfurt und Leipzig,

1710. Perry, The State of Russia, London, 1717. Korb, Diarium Itineris in Moscoviam, Vienna, 1698. Le Brun, Voyage par la Moscovie en Perse, Amsterdam, 1718. An impartial history of Peter Alexowitz, by a British officer in the service of the Czar, London, 1723. J. G. Rabener, Leben Petri des Ersten und Grossen, Leipzig, 1725. Nestesuranoi, Memoires du regne de Pierre le Grand, 1729-1737. Vita di Pietro il Grande, dall' Abbate A. Catiforo, Venezia, 1739. Peter I., by John Mottley, London, 1739. Mauvillon, Histoire de Pierre I. le Grand. Amsterdam et Leipzig, 1742. A. Gordon, The History of Peter the Great, Aberdeen, 1755. German, Leipzig, 1765. Voltaire, Histoire de l'Empire de Russie sous Pierre le Grand, Geneve, 1761-1763. German, Franckfurt und Leipzig, 1761-1764. Bacmeister, Beytrage zur Geschichte Peters des Grossen, Riga, 1774. Hupel, Nordische Miscellanen, Riga, 1782. Jacob Stahlin, Original Anekdoten von Peter dem Ersten, Leipzig, 1785. Golikow, Deeds of Peter the Great, Moskau, 1788. 30 Vols. Russian. G. A. von Halem, Leben Peters des Grossen, Munster und Leipzig, 1803-1804. J. Ch. A. Bauer, Unterhaltende Anekdoten aus dem 18. Jahrhundert Peter der Erste, Leipzig, 1804. Duncker & Humblot. B. Bergmann, Peter der Gresse als Mensch und Regent, Konigsberg und Riga, 1823-1826. Segur, Geschichte Russlands unter Peter dem Grossen, 1829. Reiche, Peter der Grosse und Seine Zeit. Pelz, Geschichte Peters des Grossen, Leipzig, 1848. Belani, Peter der Grosse, Seine Zeit und sein Hof., Leipzig, 1856. Ustrjaloff, History of the Reign of Peter the Great, St. Petersburg, 1858. Russian. Kamensky, Century of Peter the Great, St. Petersburg, 1858. Golovine, Histoire de Pierre I., Leipzig, 1861. Engelmann, Peter der Grosse, Dorpat, 1872. Pogodin, The first 17 years of the life of Peter the Great, Moscow, 1875. Russian. Barrow, Life of Peter the Great, London, 1883. Schuyler, Life of

Peter the Great, London, 1884. Hallez, Memoires secrets pour servir a l'histoire de la Russie sous les regnes de Pierre le Grand et Catherine I., Bruxelles, 1853. Memoires historiques, politiques et militaires sur la Russie, German, 1771. A select collection of singular and interesting histories, London, 1774. Le Clerc, Histoire de la Russie, Paris, 1783-1794. Merkwurdige Anekdoten aus der Geschichte Russlands bis 1736, Wien, 1787. G. A. W. von Helbig, Russische Gunstlinge, Tubingen, 1809. Maison imperiale de la Russie, Paris, 1828. La Croix, Mysteres de la Russie, Paris, 1845. Denkwurdigkeiten des Petersberger Hofes, Leipzig, 1845. Crusenstolpe, Der Russische Hof., Hamburg, 1855. Ustrjalof, History of Russia. Galitzin, La Russie au XVIII. siecle, Paris, 1863. Schlosser, Geschichte des XVIII. Jahrhunderts. Hermann, Geschichte des Russischen Staates. Peter der Grosse. Lebensbild eines Monarchen, von R. v. R., Berlin, 1869, Ssolowjef, History of Russia, Moskau, 1882. The best work on Peter is by A. Bruckner, Berlin, Grote, 1879, wherein a veil is cast over many things through which it is easy to see that the author knows more than he will tell.

CATHARINE THE FIRST AND HER LOVERS.

Catharine's Marvelous Career—Her First Lover—Her First Husband—The Mistress of Scheremetjeff, of Mentschikoff, of the Tzar — Empress—Villebois, Mons, Sapieha and Rivenvoldern.

IN looking at the marvellous career of Catharine I. it seems that only a human prodigy could have risen from so humble an estate to so dazzling a height—that chance could not have lifted any one so high. In addition to her beauty, which is said to have been seductive, Catharine was a woman of remarkable talent, of great prudence in critical moments, and of energy in pursuing her objects. A rapid glance at her career fills us with wondering admiration, but if we follow her step by step we see the flaws which the picture presents. It was the coarest sensuality which raised this peasant girl to the imperial throne.

Voltaire spoke truly when he said that she possessed none of the characteristic virtues of her sex. Shame was unknown to her.

She was the natural daughter of a Lithuanian who was, according to most writers, a serf on the estates of the Sapieha family known by the simple name of Samuel. Samuel made his escape to Dorpat, in Livonia, where all of his children were born, a son named Charles, and three daughters, Christina, Anna, and Martha, the latter on the 16th of April, 1686. The parents were Catholics, and the children were reared in that faith.

Upon Dorpat being visited by the plague Samuel fled with his family to Marienburg, in Livonia. But the pestilence on its march of triumph visited that place also, and carried off Samuel and his wife. The surviving children were cared for by charitable persons. Martha was received in the house of the minister, but he with his whole family succumbed to the epidemic, Martha alone as by a miracle surviving,

A priest named Glück, from Dunamunde, near Riga, upon learning the misfortunes which had overtaken Marienburg went to that city to do what he could toward its assistance and rescue. He visited first the pastor's house, where he found the little orphan fresh and well in the midst of the dead. Martha clung to him, called him father, and begged for something to eat. The interest and compassion of the priest were aroused, and failing after diligent inquiry to discover any family or relatives of the child, he took her to his own home. Glück remained in Marienburg.

The little guest did not meet with a very cordial welcome from Glück's wife. He persuaded her however to keep Martha, and she remained with them and was brought up in the Lutheran religion. Thus began the career of the future Empress.

As soon as the girl was old enough, she was assigned to duty with the maids. In this position Martha presented a striking contrast with her fellow-servants. Her beauty increased every day, and it was no wonder the minister's son fell in love with her. The daughters of Glück, envious of her beauty, disparaged and scorned her, and the more they did so the more ardent became the young man's devotion, and the more he felt it his duty to take the young orphan under his protection.

Months, years, passed away.

The beautiful child had grown into a captivating woman, and had already yielded her heart to her faithful lover, the pastor's son. Glück and his wife were not long in observing the intimate relation which subsisted between the two, and fearing a marriage between their son and the strange girl, they resolved to provide her with a husband. They had not long to wait for the opportunity.

A young Swedish soldier named Johann* fell in love with her and asked to marry her. Glück gladly gave his consent, and the marriage took place without delay.

They had been but three days married when the young husband was summoned to accompany his regiment to the field. The young wife again became a servant at Glück's, and in all probability renewed her relations with the son.

On the 23d of August, 1702, Marienburg was invested by the Russian colonel, Judas Boltin. The place was too weak to offer resistance, and Major Thilo, the Swedish officer in command, displayed the white flag and went to the Russian camp to surrender at discretion.

Meanwhile two other Swedish officers, Wolff

---

*According to some the name of the Swedish soldier was Johann Rabin. See Bergmann, II., 80. Golikoff, Suppl. VI, 164.

and Gottslich, one a captain the other an ensign in the artillery, determined to destroy the town and perish with it rather than surrender without resistance. They permitted the Russian troops to enter and then lighted the powder stored in the turret. A terrible explosion followed, a number of houses were destroyed and many soldiers both Russians and Swedes perished. Enraged at this act of treachery, the Russian commander gave his men license to work their will in plundering and murdering. The terrified inhabitants besought Glück to hasten to General Scheremetjeff and beg for mercy. Glück did so taking with him Martha. Her beauty attracted the attention of all, and of Scheremetjeff in particular. He paid little heed to the preacher, but kept his eyes riveted upon Martha. At last he said:

"I will forgive everything if you will give me this girl."

It was in vain that Glück represented that Martha was married. In vain that Martha had recourse to prayers and tears. The tears only heightened her beauty, and the heightened beauty increased Scheremetjeff's passion. As he refused to recede from his demand, Glück, fearing to exasperate him, surrendered Martha to him.

Martha remained only six or seven months the slave and mistress of Scheremetjeff, at the end of which time the latter delivered up his Livonian command to Prince Mentschikoff. In the course of making the exchange Mentschikoff saw Martha and begged his predecessor to relinquish her to him, and Scheremetjeff dared not refuse the request of the Tzar's all-powerful favorite.

The exchange was not unpleasing to Martha, for Scheremetjeff was old and ugly, while Mentschikoff was in the prime of manhood, good looking, gay, and lively. They lived for some time together, and Martha, though a slave the mistress of her master's heart, enjoyed in his house consideration and freedom and was perfectly happy.

But her lawful husband, the Swedish dragoon, having served his time returned home, and learning the fate of his wife hastened to her and claimed his rights. After some persuasion Martha prevailed upon him not to claim her openly but to content himself with secret visits.

Martha therefore had two husbands until Mentschikoff removed his headquarters to Livonia to unite his forces with those of the Tzar and the slave accompanied him, Johann remaining in Marienburg. Mentschikoff kept his slave carefully concealed from the eyes of the other generals, and from the Tzar.

But his jealous watchfulness was defeated when in a moment of drunken folly he boasted of possessing a mistress who was the most beautiful woman that had ever lived. Every one insisted upon seeing this marvel of creation. Mentschikoff refused to produce her, but as the Tzar insisted he was forced to consent to have her appear.

Martha came. The wine-heated assembly agreed that the boast of Mentschikoff was verified, that she was the most beautiful woman who had ever been seen. Peter at first said nothing. After awhile he stepped up to Mentschikoff and whispered something in his ear.

The favorite turned pale.

The Tzar looked at him earnestly and questioningly.

The Prince nodded assent, and Catharine's fate was sealed.

Peter turned to the young slave with some jesting remarks, to which she responded with a wit and intelligence that surprised him.

From this time the daughter of the Livonian serf remained with the Tzar, having thus swiftly and suddenly climbed to the pinnacle of human greatness.

Mentschikoff was not however left without consolation. In relinquishing his mistress to the Tzar he had not lost her heart. She remained true to him, and grateful for the happy hours she owed him. He had in her his strongest supporter, and her influence with the Tzar was solid and lasting.

Martha was installed in the palace as a servant. When in 1703, she accompanied the Tzar to Moscow, she changed again her religion and adopted the Greek faith. Peter's half-sister, Catharine, officiated as godmother, and the Tzarevitch Alexis was obliged to act the part of godfather to the mistress of Peter, who had afterwards no small share in his cruel fate. Martha received the name of Catharine Alexejevna, the combined names of Catharine and Alexis.

Together with the Russian religion she adopted the Russian language, which she quickly learned quite forgetting the Esthonian and German so that when on a visit years afterwards to the Court of Berlin she was unable to converse with the King of Prussia in his own tongue. The knowledge of the Russian language however, remained the extent of her acquirements. She never learned to read and write, and during her reign her daughter Elizabeth signed her name. Neither had she the slightest idea of arithmetic. Nevertheless she succeeded in attaching to her during his whole life a monarch so aspiring as Peter the Great.

The feature of Catharine's character which best pleased Peter was her pliancy. This was her greatest talent, the one which made her Peter's Empress, and afterwards an independent sovereign, and it was the primary cause of the lasting place which she preserved in the fancy of the fickle Tzar. The wife that suited Peter was a slave, whose subserviency never reminded him of his duty, and neither exacted nor expected constancy. Catharine's moral depravity demanded of the Tzar no respect. In the point of view of morals she was, his mate; like him, she had behind her a promiscuous past. They had therefore no cause to reproach each other. She permitted him full liberty, overlooked his former liaisons, and not only permitted new ones but even assisted in them. Thus she preserved for him her freshness ever new. After each change he returned to his Catharine, who knew how to sharpen his appetite with fresh surprises. She was full of solicitude for his already failing health, accompanied him on his most dangerous expeditions, cared for him by day and by night, and her never failing good humor rendered her society indispensable to him.

General Gordon, who held a military post under Peter and Catharine says of the latter: "Her invariable good humor made her a favorite with every one with whom she came in contact; she was never moody, or angry, or capricious."

With a view to bind the Tzar more closely to her, Catharine bribed a clergyman of Riga, by the name of Brüning, to show Peter an old document claimed to have been discovered in the archives of the city containing the prophecy, "He only can achieve the conquest of Livonia who shall wed a daughter of the land."

Although Peter was far from superstitious, this made a great impression upon him on account of the fulfilment of the prophecy. After a long and hard struggle, Livonia came into the possession of Russia, almost at the same time that Catharine came into that of Peter.

Married to her the Tzar was not yet, however. He had not dared so far to defy the customs of the land as to take a second wife while the first was still alive. Catharine at first was given a place among the Court servants, and, soon advanced to the post of nominal wife to the Court cook, which permitted her to be employed near the Emperor and to accompany him on his travels. In order completely to carry out the appearance, she occupied the cook's lodgings.

On October 28, 1707, Peter secretly married his mistress in the Cathedral of the Holy Trinity at Moscow. The mask however was soon thrown off, to which the following circumstance may have contributed:

Sometime in the year 1710, the Swedish soldier Johann was brought a prisoner to Moscow. He gave out that he was the husband of Catharine in the hope of obtaining an amelioration of his lot. But when his assertion came to the ears of Peter he banished him to the most remote regions of Siberia, where he was seen as late as the year 1721.

By this act the Tzar betrayed himself. The secret, which it was impossible longer to conceal, leaked out, and during the year 1710 Catharine began to be addressed at the Court as " Your Ladyship."

Peter was led to take the final step by a project which, although broached by Mentschikoff had been incessantly nourished, albeit prudently concealed, by Catharine, that the succession to the throne should not rest exclusively with Alexis. On the 6th of March, therefore, Peter recognized Catharine as his only, his rightful and lawful wife, and raised her children to the rank of princes and princesses.

On the same day on which this proclamation was issued, the "young pair" set out to visit the army at Moscow, which Scheremetcheff was conducting toward the Dneister to attack Moldavia by way of Poland.

As Peter could not endure a separation from Catharine she accompanied him on his foreign travels. The strange pair naturally attracted much attention at the European Courts.

If Peter himself was an object of wonder to the Continent, the slave whom he had raised to the throne was beyond belief. In the "pair of barbarians" much was found to murmur at, and not without good cause.

On the 8th of September, 1717, Peter and Catharine visited the Court of Berlin. The Margravine of Baireuth has left in her memoirs an account of this visit, which is worth reproducing:

"The Tzar," she tell us, "arrived here from Holland. He had stopped at Cleves for the lying-in of the Empress. As he was not fond of society he requested the King to permit him to occupy a pleasure house of the Queen's in a suburb of Berlin. The latter was greatly vexed.

She had built a very pretty house and furnished it with care and magnificence. It had costly galleries of porcelain, and the rooms were adorned with mirrors. The house being a little jewel it was given the name 'Monbijou.' It had a pretty garden bordering on the river, which lent to it a great attraction.

"To provide against the disorder which the Russian ladies had left behind them wherever they had been the Queen removed the costly furniture and everything which was capable of being broken.

"In a few days the Tzar and his wife and their suite arrived at Monbijou. The King and Queen received them at the river's side. The King assisted the Tzar out of the boat, and as soon as he had landed, the Tzar offered the King his hand, saying : 'I am delighted to see you, Brother Frederick.' Then he approached the Queen and was going to embrace her, but she drew back. The Tzarina kissed the Queen's hand several times. They then presented the Duke and Duchess of Mecklenburg, who had accompanied the Russian court and four hundred so-called 'ladies' of their suite. These were for the most part German servants, who performed the offices of ladies-in-waiting, chambermaids, cooks and laundresses. Almost all of them had in their arms a richly dressed child, and each, on being asked if the child was hers, answered, making her salamalaka in the Russian fashion : 'The Tzar did me the honor to make this child.'

"The Queen positively objected to saluting these creatures. The Tzarina revenged herself by treating the princesses of the blood with haughtiness, and it was with difficulty that the King could prevail on her to salute them.

"I saw the whole court on the following day when the Tzar and his wife returned the Queen's visit. The Queen received the Imperial pair in the grand apartments of the palace, going to meet them as far as the guard-room. She offered her hand to the Tzarina, and placing her on her right led her into the reception room.

"The King followed with the Tzar; the latter recognized me at once, having seen me five years before. He placed my arm in his and kissed me so violently that he scraped my whole face. I boxed his ears and defended myself as best I could, saying: 'That I could not allow such familiarities, and that they were disrespectful.' He laughed at this and talked to me a long while.

"My role had been prescribed for me in advance. I talked to him about his fleet and his conquests, which so enchanted him that he several times observed to the Tzarina that he would cheerfully give one of his provinces for a child like me. The Tzarina was also very gracious to me.

"The Queen sat by the Tzarina under the canopy of the throne, and I was near the Queen, the princesses of the blood sitting opposite to her.

"The Tzarina was small and thick-set, without nobility or grace. It was only necessary to see her to recognize her humble origin. From her dress she might have been taken for a German actress. It was purchased from a second hand dealer, was quite old-fashioned and overloaded with silver and gilt ornaments. The front of her bodice was adorned with jewels arranged in the most bizarre fashion. They represented a double eagle, the wings composed of small and very badly set brilliants. She wore a dozen orders and as many pictures of saints and relics attached to the lapel of her gown, so that when she walked she made a jingling noise that reminded one of a mule.

"The Tzar, on the other hand, was very stout and rather tall, and had a handsome face, but there was a savage look in it which made one afraid He was dressed quite simply, like a sailor.

"When the company went to the table the Tzar was seated next the Queen. Owing to having been poisoned in his youth he suffered from a nervous affection which showed itself in a species of cramp. He was seized with one of these attacks at the table. A convulsion came on as he held his knife in his hand, and he flourished it close to the Queen, who sprang up in alarm. He quieted her and begged her to remain seated, assuring her that he would do her no harm. The next instant he seized her hand and squeezed it so violently that she was obliged to beg for mercy, whereupon the Tzar laughed, and said she had as tender knuckles as his Catharine.

"After supper all began preparation for a ball except the Tzar, who as soon as he arose from the table departed, returning on foot to Monbijou.

"The next day there were pointed out to him the objects of interest in Berlin, among others the mint office and some antique statuary. Among the statues was one which exhibited a heathen divinity in a very indecent posture. In the days of the old Romans such representations were used as decorations for the bridal chamber. It was one of the rarest and most beautiful of these ancient statues. The Tzar was filled with admiration, and told the Tzarina to kiss it. She tried to refuse, whereupon he became very angry, and said in broken German: 'Kopp ab!' which was equivalent to, 'I will have you beheaded if you do not obey me.' The Tzarina, terrified, did as he directed.

"The next thing the Tzar did was to ask that the statue be presented to him. The request could not be refused, and it was accompanied by a small table with a wainscoting of amber. This was something quite unique of its kind, and had cost Frederick I. an enormous sum of money. Its sad destiny, to the regret of everyone, was to be sent to St. Petersburg.

"At the end of two days this barbaric court took its departure. The Queen immediately set out for Monbijou, where another destruction of Jerusalen had been in progress. Never have I seen anything to equal it. Everything was in such a state of complete ruin that the whole house had to be refitted."

So much for the Margravine of Baireuth. The truth of her description has, as might be expected, been warmly disputed by Russian authors.

Granting however that the Princess Frederica has drawn too shocking a picture in her account of the four hundred "ladies;" or of the statue, it must be acknowledged that the manners of the Russian Court were well fitted to offend the least fastidious. Even so sober an historian as Schlosser utters this condemnation:

"Even in Prussia, and in presence of the Court, Peter permitted himself in familiarities with his niece, the Duchess of Mecklenburg, which could not be recited, and which, in the presence of others, would shame the rudest of barbarians."

Catharine became every day more dear to Peter. Her well-known exploit at Pruth especially won for her his favor and approbation.

Peter and his army were hemmed in in a desert country by an overwhelming Turkish force, and there seemed no way for him to extricate himself with honor. The choice was between starvation and surrender. Under these circumstances Catharine conceived the project of going in person to the enemy's camp and bribing the Grand Vizier. Collecting together all her own jewels she went from camp to camp and begged from officers and soldiers every valuable object they would surrender.

The Grand Vizier, won by the gold and jewels, as well as by the beauty of Catharine, granted the Russians a passage.

When Peter was informed of Catharine's act he did not know how to be grateful enough. On his return from the war he created the order of Catharine and put aside the unlucky Alexis in favor of Catharine's son Peter. As, however, the latter died in early childhood, the Tzar chose Catharine as his successor and in 1724 her coronation took place in Moscow. This design Mentschikoff had earnestly encouraged, although Jaguschinski, a favorite, who went by the name of * "The Tzar's Eye,"

---

* Paul Jaguschinski, one of the most interesting of the favorites of Peter, was born in Moscow in 1583. His father was sacristan of the German-Lutheran Church there. In his eighteenth year Paul had the good fortune to become known to Peter I., and by his apt replies to win the favor of that Prince. He soon after adopted the Greek faith. Peter gave him a place in the Imperial

and who in the latter part of Peter's reign enjoyed the greatest consideration, even obscuring for a time the favor of Mentschikoff, strongly opposed it.

He also gave way at last, however, and the coronation took place in May. But it was no sooner accomplished than Peter had cause to repent that he had listened to Mentschikoff rather than to Jaguschinski, for his love and confidence were ill requited.

Chancellery, where he remained for some years and won great ecomium. He was afterwards transferred to the Guards, and thus brought in close contact with the Tzar, whose good graces he very soon won. He was one of those who, in 1717, signed the sentence of death of the unhappy Alexis. Four years later he was made Procurator General in the Senate, where, in the Emperor's name, he exercised a too controlling and the only decisive influence. After Peter's death he went over to the Empress, became her ardent supporter, and was rewarded for his fickleness with the rank of count. Toward the close of Catharine's reign he fell into disgrace on accout of a difference with Mentschikoff. He outlasted his opponent, however, Mentschikoff being exiled in the reign of Peter II., and after Peter's death he was a member of the High Assembly which chose his successor. On the accession of the Empress Anna, this Assembly ordered his arrest because he counseled the new sovereign to violate the liberal capitulations and to reign like her predecessors, arbitrarily. The gratitude of the Empress, however, saved him. This was the first act of absolutism performed by Anna, who had bound herself to govern constitutionally and who owed her elevation to

It seemed as though there was no end to the trials of Peter toward the close of his life. He saw his house orphaned, himself without an heir. Of his seven children, his sons died in early youth, and all hope of seeing the structure which he had reared preserved and extended by a son of his own, educated with that view, had been dashed to the ground. Seeing himself threatened with the subversion of the purposes to which his life had been

the throne to this oath. Jaguschinski again became Procurator General. He fell out, however, with Biron, and even drew his sword upon the powerful favorite of the Empress. It is something to be wondered at and bears strong testimony to Anna's grateful disposition that she permitted him to go unpunished, merely sending the too pugnacious Jaguschinski as Ambassador to Berlin. When she thought his hot blood had had time to cool, she recalled him, and made him a Minister in her Cabinet. He died in 1736, and was interred in the monastery of Newsky, where his epitaph may be seen in the first church on the left hand at the entrance to the cloister. Jaguschinski was one of those as to whose intelligence the Tzar did not err. He was a man of extraordinary ability and of an ingenuous character. He and Repnine were almost the only persons who were accustomed to speak the unvarnished truth to Peter the Great. Unfortunately, his disposition was violent and his love of drink incorrigible. Jaguschinski was twice married. His first wife he repudiated, the second was a Countess Golowkin. Of the princely race which sprang from the son of the sacristan it is not possible here to give an account.

devoted by his own son, he had sent him to his death, but in putting to death his son he had not extinguished the discontent which he had aroused among a people who were unripe for the civilization he had thrust upon them, and which had forced him, the great Tzar of the Russians, to surround himself with foreigners, and to entrust to them the highest and most confidential posts in the Empire. Instead of love he had earned hate, instead of admiration and recognition, fear and contumacy.

The few friends he had won during his life, the favorites whom he had taken from the dregs of the people and raised to the highest dignities, showed themselves at last, false and unworthy of his trust. He had to tear them out of his heart, to cast them out of his presence, to deliver them to the executioner, to banish them into exile.

To crown all he was seized with a frightful malady which distracted him with agony, which martyred and tortured him more terribly than he had martyred his son, or his worst enemies or antagonists. But all this had come upon him as the consequence of his own misdeeds, an unbroken chain of cause and effect

The terrible malady which tormented his

soul and body was a consequence of his drunken excesses, and his unbridled licenciousness. The faithlessness of his officials and favorites was induced by his contempt of the opinions of others, and the cruel punishments which he inflicted upon all who differed from him. The reprobation and hatred of his subjects he had earned by his savage violence, and his despotic resolve to brook no delay in the execution of his behests. The early death of his children he owed to his brutality toward the Tzarina, even in the moment when her hour of trial was near. Finally, he had turned against him his son by his unworthy treatment of Eudoxia. The mother's hatred for her tormentor was bred in the child who as he advanced in years groaned under his despotism, and who, when he grew old enough to think, struggled to break the chains which oppressed him and to avenge her wrongs.

How dark, how gloomy, all now is about the Tzar! The blackest clouds on the horizon have rolled together; damply and heavily pants the wind; sharp flashes quiver in the heavens, and at last on the forsaken Emperor the storm bursts forth. The day of vengeance for all the Tzar's wild lust has come, retribution for the bitter grief of Eudoxia, of Anna Mons,—and it is a brother of the last who is the instrument of retributive justice.

Full is the cup of sin, full the cup of remorse.

There lived in the capital a handsome young man, Mons de la Croix, a brother of Anna Mons and of the wife of General Balk. Peter, who liked the company of foreigners, fancied the young man and often invited him to the palace. Catherine saw him and became enamoured of his beauty. She drew him on and even brought him to be in love with her. In order to make it easy for them to meet, she secured him a position near her. At her instance Peter unsuspectingly appointed him first a gentleman of the bedchamber, and then chamberlain to the Empress.

For several years their intimacy continued, quiet and unnoticed. But the secret was at last betrayed, and the piquant tale was whispered louder and louder until it reached the Tzar's ear. He refused to believe it, and remained unconcerned. But as more urgent warnings were brought to him, he bethought him of his former mistress, who was the sister of Mons and able therefore to keep an eye upon him. He commissioned her to examine into the facts of the supposed connection and to learn the truth.

Madame Balk made the terrible discovery that the relation did, in fact, exist.

She hesitated long between her affection for her brother and her obedience to the Tzar. At last the former feeling prevailed, and she resolved to incur the most severe punishment sooner than cause the ruin of her brother.

The court was then at Peterhof, near St. Petersburg.

The 8th of November, 1724, the Tzar feigned to go on a journey. Scarcely, however, had he left the palace than he returned, entered it unobserved and surprised the Tzarina and Mons together in a chamber.

What happened is not to be described.

When his first paroxysm of wrath had spent itself, during which he beat Catherine until she bled, he stormed into the adjacent room occupied by Prince Repnin, his Adjutant General.

It was two hours past midnight.

Repnin sprang up upon Peter's entrance. The Tzar's fists were clenched and his whole frame shook; his face was distorted like a maniac's, his eyes glared with rage.

Repnin was confounded; he thought the Tzar had come to beat him. He dared not stir.

Peter gasped: "Get up; I wish to speak to you."

Then he informed him of his terrible discovery.

"I must have vengeance, a terrible vengeance; I will murder the Tzarina."

For a while Repnin stood helpless and speechless in presence of the Tzar's wrath. After a while, however, he sought to soothe him. He agreed that no punishment was great enough for Catherine's fault, but begged him to bear in mind that he could not deal with the Tzarina as with an ordinary woman; reminded him of the streltzi's bath of blood, of the cruel executions that since that year had stained the land, of the imprisonment of his half sister Sophia, of the Tzarina Eudoxia, and of the death of Alexis, which had excited malicious comments abroad. If now he were to repudiate or execute a second wife, his great deeds would be forgotten and the only name by which he would be known, would be that of a bloodthirsty tyrant.

At first Peter glowered threateningly at the bold speaker, but as Repnin, unabashed, proceeded to sum up his remarks, the Tzar sank down, crushed and trembling.

For a long time he sat motionless at the Prince's bedside.

Then he rose, went to his chamber without a word, and walked to and fro. He decided at last to follow the counsels of Repnin. He would make a show of sparing Catharine, but the brother and sister Mons must perish.

The sentence of the latter was executed the next day. She was knouted and exiled to Siberia, whence she seems never to have returned, although Catharine, through whom this misfortune had befallen her, two months after ascended the throne.

Mons was arrested under a charge of "having embezzled money belonging to the Empress," * and taken to the house of Uschakoff, the President of the Secret Chancellery, and, after being kept there two days without food, was brought before the highest court, which held its sittings in the Winter Palace, and very shortly after beheaded.

In order so far as possible to exculpate Catharine, Mons gave out that he had seduced her by charms and philters.

---

* Professor Brückner, who passes over this event which he says rests upon unverified probabilities, with a few lines (Peter der Grosse, Seite 564, Anmerkung 5), expresses his opinion that "there is no doubt that Mons was guilty of dishonesty and bribery." Compare also Ssolowjeff, XVIII., 245. Kostomaroff (in the Russian periodical "Old and New Russia," 1877, 1, 149) attempts to set forth the improbability of Catharine's infidelity.

Mons was a Lutheran, and on being carried to the scaffold he requested to be allowed to see a minister of that faith. He covertly placed in his hands a watch which contained his name and that of the Empress in a monogram. It was a present from Catharine.

On the scaffold he bethought him of still another memento of Catharine which he carried about him and of which the discovery might lead to unfortunate consequences. He bent over and whispered in the executioner's ear. Everyone supposed he was asking for a speedy death.

"In my clothing you will find a picture set with costly diamonds. Keep the diamonds and destroy the picture." The sentence was then executed.

The executioner complied with the request to destroy the picture of the Empress.

After the execution of Mons, which Catharine was required by the Tzar to witness, the imperial pair returned to the palace. The Empress, to all appearance calm and indifferent, retired to her room. The Emperor entered with violence and with an air so terrible that Catharine thought her last hour had struck. Peter was deathly pale. He jerked his hunting knife out of its sheath and rushed toward his wife, who staggered backward, and the Tzar's wrath fell upon the furniture, the tables, chairs and window. This lasted a half-hour, after which he rushed out of the room.

The next morning he approached the Empress calmly and desired her to drive with him. He himself held the reins. All of a sudden they found themselves confronting the head and body of the executed man, which were placed upon poles. The Tzar drove so close to them that Catharine's gown grazed the corpse.

After he had continued this cruelty for some time without causing any emotion in the Empress, he turned back.

That same evening he brought the head of Mons to the Empress, and forced her to have it before her eyes for several days. He then presented it to the Academy of Sciences to be preserved with the head of Miss Hamilton.

Sixty years after, the Princess Dashkoff, the "President" of the Academy of Sciences remarked that, on looking through the accounts of the institution she observed that there had been made every year an entry for spirits "for two heads in the cellar." She searched, and found the heads of Miss Hamilton and Mons, which were so well preserved that one could not but be struck with their extraordinary beauty. By an order of the then Empress, Catharine II., the two heads were interred in the cellar.

After this terrible event Peter never again spoke to Catharine. He separated from her, and every effort to soften him proved vain. The Princess Kantemir succeeded her in the Tzar's favor. Mentschikoff, also, suffered from the disgrace into which Catharine had fallen, as Peter accused him of having an understanding with her. Their fate hung in the balance, for the Tzar threatened to cast them both back into the dust out of which he had lifted them so high. But at this time Peter the Great fell ill, and Catharine and Mentschikoff took care that he did not recover. On the 28th of January, 1725, the greatest of Russian rulers died, and the slave-born Martha ascended the throne of the Romanoffs as Catharine I. It was known that Peter before his death had intended to exclude her from the succession, but the Empress bribed the famous metropolitan, Theophanes, to swear in front of the army that Peter had said to him on his death-bed: "Catharine alone is worthy to reign." And the Russian people, always good-natured, suffered themselves to be persuaded and bowed their heads meekly.

Catharine now reigned in her own right, and needed not to consider any man. She gave free reign to her passionate nature, and not only maintained open relations with Mentschikoff but with other lovers, among whom may be specially mentioned the Counts Sapieha and Rivenvoldern. Sapieha was young and handsome, and for a time she was devoted to him. When she grew tired of him she married him to her niece, the Countess Skavronska. Rivenvoldern preserved her favor longer than Sapieha—he preserved it during eight whole months.

The reign of Catharine was short and was nominal only. It was Mentschikoff who reigned.

She was about to rouse herself and shake off his yoke when she fell ill and died in a few days. According to some historians, Catharine died of consumption and dropsy, induced by drink. According to others, hers was not a natural death. She was accustomed to receive presents of bonbons from gentlemen of her court, and one day Mentschikoff, it is said, had the politeness to present her with some very choice confections ′ . . . .

THE MARRIAGE AND THE LOVE AFFAIR OF THE TZAREVITCH ALEXIS.

The Tzarevitch Alexis, the Son of Eudoxia.—His Neglected Education.—His Marriage to a Princess of Brunswick.—His Harshness to His Wife and His Love for a Finland Serf.

FROM his earliest childhood the Tzarevitch Alexis had known nothing but misfortune. He was only eight years old when his mother, Eudoxia Lopuchina, Peter the Great's first wife, was cruelly cast off. Her disgrace had an unfavorable effect upon the relations to each other of father and son. The little Alexis aroused no very affectionate feelings in the breast of Peter, who willing to banish disagreeable memories suffered the heir to the throne in his presence as little as possible.

Is it to be wondered at if he, on his part, found in his heart little love for his father, only grief for the loss of his mother and for her ill treatment, or that the feeling grew into a deep-rooted thirst for vengeance?

When the Prince reached his tenth year Peter awakened to the idea that the successor to the throne, the heir of a great and powerful empire, should be provided with an education, and a German baron named Huyssen was appointed tutor and governor to the Tzarevitch, with Mentschikoff as his supervisor. The consequence was that whatever benefit Huyssen sought to confer, Mentschikoff endeavored to counteract. The Prince, therefore, made little progress, while his character was weakened and misshapen. And yet he was not without parts.*

---

*"Alexis," so wrote Baron Huyssen, "is a Prince whose mind is capable of grasping anything. He devotes three hours a day to his studies. He has already read the Bible through six times in Slavonic and once in German, and all the Greek fathers, besides going rapidly through other books, religious and secular, which have been published in Moscow, Kiev and Wallachia. He writes and speaks German and French well. Every day he learns something by heart, studies intelligently the lives of emperors and kings, and wishes to emulate their great deeds. Mathematics and bodily exercises have not been overlooked. Briefly, Alexis is a gentleman who fears God, has a child's respect and obedience for his father, a particular consideration for home and foreign ministers and a thoughtful affection for his servants and subjects."

Alexis had a special bias toward theological studies. His copy of theological works was filled with commentaries in his own handwriting. He shrank from worldly affairs, and as far as possible shunned the amusements of the Court. If compelled to be present he took no part in conversations relating to war and politics, but escaping with some priests into a corner discussed subjects relating to the church.

Baron Huyssen endeavored to counteract this pernicious narrowness of mind, but vainly, for Mentschikoff opposed his efforts and took pains to have Alexis kept in ignorance of affairs of state. When Huyssen attempted to stand upon his rights as governor and tutor, Mentschikoff got rid of the troublesome professor by despatching him on a mission from the Court.

Mentschikoff had now the game in his own hands, and his well-known ignorance of reading and writing did not prevent him from assuming the whole charge of the Prince's education. This education consisted in a careful suppression of any interest which the Prince might exhibit in affairs of state. He permitted him freely to follow his theological bent, and allowed him the fullest opportunity for the indulgence of his sensual passions, this being the surest road to ruin. Alexis made the best use of his opportunities. He was not only the most devout; he was also the most dissolute young man of his time.

Mentschikoff's severe discipline, which did not hesitate to show itself in action, was not fitted to strengthen or improve the character of the Tzarevitch. The least failure in submission to his cruel tutor was punished with severity. The boy's soul was consumed with helpless rage at seeing himself compelled to endure such oppression at the hands of the upstart who had brought about the ruin of his mother. If he dared to fly to his father for rescue, the Tzar roughly repulsed him; he "had no time,"—for Peter had time only for his wars, his world-stirring innovations, his amours; he had no time for his son.

And after such an attempt to obtain justice and protection, Alexis had reason to dread the worst from Mentschikoff.

Thus year after year passed, and thus Alexis grew up, more wretched than the poorest peasant's son. The Prince was yet but a boy when the star of the slave girl, who, under Mentschikoff's protection sped on her marvellous career with dizzy speed, appeared on the horizon. Her influence was not long in being felt at Court, and with such protection as the powerful favorite now enjoyed in his protégée, his conduct to the Tzarevitch grew more than ever haughty and overbearing. And when at last the incredible happened, and the low-born girl ascended the throne of Russia, and the probability increased of the birth of a prince to Peter by his new marriage—a prince more worthy in their eyes—then, indeed, all was lost.

The marriage of Peter to his paramour Catharine, at whose baptism Alexis had been forced to act as godfather, inflicted a cruel wound of which the nobles and clergy availed themselves to whisper temptation in his ear. They detested Peter and the innovations by which they had been shorn of their power. All their hopes, therefore, were centered upon Alexis, whom they strove to win to their cause. They held up before him the dangers to himself from Catharine's elevation, represented to him that the Tzar desired only his destruction, and that the destiny that awaited him was to be repudiated like his mother.

Then Alexis saw that his youth, his happiness, his life were destroyed. And he would not perish, he would not be destroyed. He listened to the whisperers for he knew they whispered the truth, and turning his back on the father who had neglected, imbittered and destroyed him, he threw himself into the hands of the Tzar's enemies. And Mentschikoff exulted, for all this was not concealed from him. He exulted that the hated Tzarevitch should dig his own grave, and hastened to denounce and expose him to the Tzar.

Peter was startled. He perceived the abyss that yawned at his feet. He realized his fault and that he had himself plunged his only son and the heir to the throne into ruin, and had made him a traitor to his father and sovereign.

Remorse took possession of him; he would fain at last have atoned for the errors of which he had been guilty. He summoned his son, expostulated with him, warned him, pointed out the wrong he was committing and its fatal consequences. He kept him near him, exerted himself to reform him, but—it was too late. Alexis was obdurate, and even though the Tzar placed for a time the government in his hands he continued unmoved, and availed himself of the opportunity to serve and benefit his friends and his father's enemies.

Grief and rage took possession of the Tzar, but conscious how greatly he was to blame for the disloyalty of Alexis, he refrained from inflicting upon him severe punishment. As a last expedient for reclaiming the prince he resolved to marry him to a foreign princess, to send him abroad for a time to learn foreign habits and customs, and thereby to enlighten his mind, change his feelings and strengthen his character.

The Tzar's choice fell upon the beautiful Princess Charlotte of Brunswick. The Tzarevitch made no opposition to the project. Attached though he perhaps was to the custom of his forefathers of taking a Russian bride, he hoped through his marriage with a foreign princess to win back his father's favor and secure the succession to the throne.

The Princess Charlotte was the second daughter of Anton Ulrich, and the youngest sister of the wife of the Emperor Charles VI. She was beautiful in person and possessed every mental gift that could permanently attach the heart of a man. It was Baron Huyssen who brought about the marriage, and he also obtained permission for the princess to adhere to the Lutheran faith.

On the 14-25 of October, 1711, the marriage was celebrated at Taugau with great magnificence.*

---

*A medal representing the marriage of the Tzarevitch and the Princess shows a bust likeness of the pair with the inscription Alex. Petr. Imp. Russ. Haer. et Carol.

Peter's plan seemed at first to promise success, but it proved delusive. Scarcely had Alexis returned to Russia than every good result of the marriage disappeared and the old passions regained the mastery. Princess Charlotte clung to him tenderly and tried with love and

---

Christ. Soph. Pr. Bruns. et Lun. R. An altar with a fire burning on it and two coats of arms, the Russian Eagle and the horse of the house of Brunswick. On the altar two joined hands with the inscription: Non usquam junxit nobiliora fides. On the rim: Ob nupt. Torgau celebrat. XXV. Oct. MDCCXI.

The Helmstadt Professor Johan Georg Eckhard proved on the occasion of this marriage that the bridal pair were both of them descended from the Greek Emperor Constantine. "Heaven itself," observed this learned Professor, "seemed to sanction the project of marriage and to guide the feet of the white dove, which, lighting on to the castle of Wolfenbüttel and sitting upon the globe of the earth which stood there, pointed thoughtfully with its feet to the Atlantic Ocean and Muscovite Tartary, just as the parents of the affianced Princess were taking counsel together on the destiny of their illustrious house."

Adverting to this pretty conceit Anton Ulrich, the father of the bride, said: "This event could furnish the material for a history." The philosopher Leibnitz made the following epigram upon it:

Augurium columbae.
Blankenburgiaci museo in Principis, Orbem
Signat olivifero laeta columba pede.
Hinc Scythiae in campis, illinc Atlantis in undis.
Scilicet et Natas utraque regna colent.
(Leibnitii Literae ed. Chr. Kortholt, I, 286.)

goodness to work upon him, but she could obtain no influence; nor did Alexis, even after she had become a mother, cease to be insensible, hard and repellant.

Peter, who held his noble daughter-in-law in high esteem, was exasperated by the conduct of Alexis, but his reproaches only provoked his son's opposition. He abandoned his wife and gave himself up to the wildest excesses. And Peter dared not reproach him, for the son could with justice appeal to the father's example. Following in the footsteps of the Tzar, Alexis fell madly in love with a peasant girl of Finland, whose career however as compared with that of Catherine was blameless. Her name was Euphrosyne, and she was beautiful. She accompanied him upon his flight into Germany, was arrested and brought back to Russia, appeared before the Tzar, and was pardoned by him upon her proving to him that she had not sought to entrap Alexis but had been forced by threats of personal violence to live with him. Peter made her valuable presents, and promised her a handsome portion if she would marry. But she answered, "I was constrained to a first love, I will never of my free will belong to another man."

The wife of Alexis was inconsolable over this event. She died heart-broken on the 20th of October, 1715, shortly after having given birth to a son, Peter, the future Emperor.

The love of Alexis for the peasant girl Euphrosyne, cost the Princess her life, and was also one of the causes which led to the death of the Tzarevitch.

The death of the Princess and the circumstance that a few days after, Catharine was delivered of a son, who received the name of Peter, induced the Tzar to cast off his heir, and the last link between father and son, between Emperor and Crown Prince, was severed. The only wonder is that the insupportable relations between them had lasted two years.

On the 3d of February, 1718, the Tzar issued a manifesto in which he declared Alexis to have forfeited his right to the succession and set forth the incurable perverseness of his character. He was brought to trial and delivered to a violent death.

The manifesto in which Peter gave notice to his subjects of the dispossession of the heir to the throne, is an interesting document. In it the Tzar describes the conduct of his son from his earliest years. He refers to the impossibility of imparting to him an education, and complains of his association with evil men from whom neither indulgence nor severity had been able to detach him. "To teach him the art of war," he continues, "I have had him accompany me on my campaigns, protecting him from dangers to which I did not hesitate to expose myself. To instruct him in the art of government I have intrusted him with the regency. To arouse him to emulation I have sent him into foreign lands; but all my efforts have been as seed falling upon a rock. Not only has he refused to love the good, he has hated it. He married a Princess of his own choice, intelligent, gifted, and virtuous, but far from reforming, he violated his marriage vows for the sake of a woman of low birth with whom he openly lived, and by so doing has shortened the life of his wife. Lastly, by his flight, he has filled up the measure of his crimes. He has placed himself under the protection of the Emperor Charles, and with slanderous charges that I persecute him and without cause have excluded him from the succession, and that his life is not safe near me, he has requested armed protection for his person. He has refused to return, and was finally induced to do so only by the fear of being delivered up against his will. He has himself acknowledged his guilt. He has well deserved death. But paternal affection has compassion on him. I pardon his crime and release him from all punishment therefor. But to permit this unworthy Prince to succeed me is against my conscience, for I foresee that by his pernicious conduct he will destroy the glory of the nation, will lose the provinces which I have won by my unwearied efforts, and by the grace of God have made secure, will break up the scientific institutions which I have with pains established for the fame and welfare of the Empire. My subjects would be objects of pity did I abandon them to such a successor, to be thrown backward into a condition worse than the previous one. Therefore, for the welfare of my Empire and exercising the paternal authority which by the laws of the country every private citizen possesses of disinheriting his son, as well as by my sovereign will, I declare my son Alexis, both by reason of his crime and by his unworthiness to reign, to have forfeited his rights as heir to the throne, even the case arising that I should have no other offspring. And as I have no son who is more advanced in years, I declare my second son Peter, notwithstanding his youth the heir to the throne. My paternal curse will rest upon Alexis if he should ever claim or seek to succeed me. My subjects of every degree shall, according to this my ordinance, respect the rights of my son Peter to the succession, and any person who at a future day, shall recognize Alexis as my heir, and shall lend him aid to seize the reins of this Empire, I declare a traitor to myself and to his country." (See Reports of the trials of the Tzarvitch Alexis. 1718.—A. Brückner. Alexis. Heidelberg, 1880.)

With regard to the manner of the Tzarevitch's death every variety of report has been current. Ustrjalof takes the view that he died in consequence of knouting, asserting that he was given forty strokes of the knout, one of which would have been sufficient to cause death. Pleyer (see Ustrjalof VI, 541-545), speaks of the Prince as having been beheaded. This tradition has remained the strongest, though with very varying details. Generally, Adam Weide and Anna Kramer have been made to perform a part in it. Compare Busching IX preface. Dolgaruckow I, 10. Helbig 69 and 71. De Bie wrote to the States General that Alexis had been killed by the opening of a vein. (Ustrjalof VI, 549-569). Lefort, the Saxon Minister maintained that Peter himself knouted his son to death. Bruce and another writer, von Rumjantzoff, talk of poison. The poisoning of the heir to the throne is also spoken of in "A Select Collection" II, 123. Compare also, "The Tzarevitch Alexis Petrovitch," from newly discovered sources, in the journal of the Russian Historical society, 1861, III. Duclos, *Pieces Interessantes et Peu Connues,* 130. Bulau "Geheime Geschichten und rätselhafte Menschen," Leipsig, Brockhaus, 1863, Vol. IV, 161-184

THE CHILDREN OF PETER THE GREAT AND CATHARINE THE FIRST.

Domestic life of the imperial pair.—Correspondence.—Peter Petrovitch, heir to the throne after the death of Alexis.—His tragic end.—The Princess Anna.—A melodramatic love story.

CATHARINE bore the Tzar seven children: Prince Peter, Princess Anna, who as the Duchess of Holstein became the mother of Peter III, Princess Elizabeth afterwards Empress of Russia, three other daughters and a son who died young.

As a family they lived together not unamiably. The letters of Peter to Catharine bear witness to this. Catherine could only answer them however, by the aid of her children and the ladies of her court.* In Peter's letters a

---

*This correspondence was first published by the "Commission to Edit the State Papers and Treaties in the Archives of the ministry of Foreign Relations at

jocular tone prevails. Here and there, however, very serious matters are touched upon, in which Catharine shows no lack of interest; the cares of business, the dangers likely to arise out of political developments, the high stake played for in the Northern war. He sighs over the burden of his responsibilities, and in 1712 writes: "Thank God we are safe, but it is a hard life. I can do little with my left hand and my right must wield both pen and sword. How much help I get, you know full well."

The Tzarina understood, and sought to enliven him. She never let pass an opportunity to do so. Upon every anniversary of the least of his victories, she congratulated him. She followed with the most intense interest the vicisitudes of his campaigns, even taking note of their details, and made arrangements for appro-

---

Moscow," as Part I of the "Letters of Russian Rulers and the Members of their Families," Moscow, 1861, page 166. The volume contains 223 letters, 173 of Peter's and 50 of Catharine's, 1707-1724. A full narrative, more systematic and clearer than the original edition, is the "Historical Almanac," published by A. Brückner in Raumer-Riehl, 1880, 173-239. Compare also: Brückner, Peter der Grosse, Berlin, 1879, 568. Collection of Letters of Peter the First, Petersburg, 1829. Letters and documents of Peter the Great, Petersburg, 1887-1889. The works of Golikof, Ustrjalof and Ssolowjef.

priate celebrations of his victories in the city and Empire. She was also fully alive to the significance of Peter's darling creation, his fleet, rejoiced in the increase of his squadrons, watched the progress of the ship-building and herself presided over the trials. She never forgot to make flattering observations to the Tzar, and by these methods was able to keep his affection for her ever warm.

Peter wrote often to the Tzarina, and always when in movement, if only a few lines as a sign of life. The letters are valuable and interesting. When he wrote to her to come to him, he gave the most minute directions and begged her to beware of unnecessarily fatiguing herself.

Until the year 1712 the letters were addressed "To Katharina Alexejewna," after she was officially proclaimed the wife of the Emperor "To the Gossudarynja Zarin Katharina Alexejewna." Letters from foreign countries usually bore only the address: "a sa Majesté la Czarinne." His manner of addressing herself is also chronological. From 1707 to 1709 he calls her Matka, mother. From 1711 the letters begin "mother, good morning," or "Muder," in Russian characters; or "Katharinuschka, my friend, I salute you, friend of my heart."

The style of Catharine's address in her letters to the Tzar is more reverential. She begins, "Your Grace," or "Your Majesty," but as her letters progress she grows warmer: "My little father," "my heart's friend," "my friend," "my Lord Vice Admiral, I hope you are well, many years to you," and once the somewhat mystical, "Most Illustrious, Distinguished August Prince, Master and Knight of the Grand Circles, and of Life and Death, Excellency."

In his letters to Catharine Peter appears only as a good-natured, smooth-tongued lover. Once in 1808 he says, "I hope, mother, to see you soon, it is dull and gloomy without you. There is no one here to look after my washing." From Wolgast, on the 14th of August, 1712: "I arrived here to-day with the fleet, and hope soon to be with you; I long greatly to see you and I believe you are still more impatient, but it must be endured a little longer, then our meeting will be all the more joyful." And in 1716: "Without you it is far too dreary, that you know full well; to be at so short a distance and not to see each other." He begs her "for God's sake" to write to him oftener. With his letters he sent her little presents, stuff for her gowns, lemons, a watch "after the newest fashion, with a glass to keep the dust from penetrating," oysters, Hungarian wine from Poltawa; in Belgium he bought her the most beautiful lace, "more beautiful than can be found anywhere else in Europe;" upon having his hair cut at Revel he sent her the cut off hair. Once he sent her a fox and a pair of doves, at another time strawberries and cherries, beer, oranges and cucumbers.

She answered these presents generally with drinks, especially brandy, also fruits and nuts, once a barrel of herring, at another time in 1717 a waistcoat to Spaa, the first worn by Peter. To Paris a flask of Hungarian wine with the remark: "Were I with Your Majesty we should, I think, not need so much Hungarian wine." In 1717 Peter wrote to her: "I thank you for your present and send one to you; very appropriate presents on both sides. You send me that wherewith to sustain my old age, I send you something with which to adorn your youth." In reply she scolded him roundly for calling himself "an old fellow" and offered to produce witnesses to the falsity of such an assertion. In the letters much mention is made of "Iwaschka Chmelnizky," the Russian name for Bacchus. The Tzar tells of his adventures with this jolly companion, and Catharine entering into the humor, writes: "The

Frenchman who is arranging a new garden was passing along a ditch when Iwaschka Chmelnizky gave him a lunge and sent him to make flower beds in another world."

Peter very rarely alludes to his impressions of foreign countries. He wrote from Carlsbad in 1711: "Here we are, thank God, quite well, somewhat inflated with much drinking. They water us like horses, there is nothing else here to do." There is no lack of bold jests, sometimes frivolous, sometimes cynical. In 1709 she warned him against love adventures, and he answered, "we are old people, and not such —." She attaches no importance to his "little love affairs" if he continues true to her.

For Catharine's children also, Peter evinces a warmth of sympathy and affection in strong contrast with his conduct to Alexis. In this correspondence the name of Alexis is scarcely mentioned. In 1711 Peter writes from Torgau of the betrothal of the Tzarevitch to the Princess Wolfenbüttel, and adds: "I congratulate you on your new daughter-in-law." In 1714 the Tzarina remarks that a letter has been received from Alexis which she encloses. That is all. After the catastrophe of 1718, however, mention is sometimes made of the children of Alexis. In a letter of October

1718, Peter says that the birthday of his three year old grandson must be celebrated with a "collation." On one occasion Catharine mentions that she and the children "and grandchildren" are well.

The birthdays and christening days of the children were never forgotten. Peter listened with pleasure to Catharine's accounts of them, their sayings and doings. When they were ill the Tzar showed the utmost concern. His pet expression for them is singular enough. "Kiss my entrails for me," he often says. And later he wrote to wife and children together. "Katharinuschka, my heart's friend, I salute both you and the entrails." To his two oldest daughters he gushes on this wise: "Annuschka and Lisenka, I salute you. Thank you for your letters. God be with you." Sometimes he jestingly calls his daughters "suckers."*

---

*In 1771 the German Ambassador Bergholz came to Petersburg, and he has thus described the Empress and her family:

It was in the broad central garden walk that we saw the Empress in the neighborhood of a pretty fountain, very splendidly dressed. The eldest Princess, Anna, first drew my attention. She is a brunette as pretty as an angel, has the prettiest complexion, hands and figure in the world. She resembles the Tzar very much and is already tall for a woman. On the Tzarina's left was the second princess. Elizabeth, who has blonde hair, a pretty

The favorite of the parents was little Prince Peter Petrovitch. His birth had thrown the Tzar into a transport of delight. It happened at the time when his relations with Alexis were at their worst. The Tzar now saw his throne and the succession no longer dependent upon one pair of eyes, those of the refractory Alexis. He had now a son whom he could train

---

complexion, and a face as charming as her elder sister's, with much greater animation and vivacity. She is almost two years younger and is much smaller, but her throat and bust are fuller, those of the elder being quite thin, and dresses more girlishly, although both wore gowns laced in the back which were exceedingly well made. Their hair was ornamented with a number of jewels and arranged according to the latest French fashion, and as well as if they had the best French coiffuese. The little Grand Duke Peter Alexejvitch and his sister Natalia, the children of the late Princess of Wolfenbuttel and the late Crown Prince, stood near the Empress, and I must say these two children looked as they were moulded in wax, and were as pretty as angels. The Prince is six years old and well grown for his years, the Princess is nearly eight and is not small for her age. These two have their own table apart, and the two Princesses have theirs. The little four year old daughter of the Empress is carried in the arms, and is a remarkably pretty child. The old Tzarina (widow of the late Tzar Ivan), with her daughter, four years old, a brunette and not ill looking, was also there. Among the other ladies whom I saw, the Princess Tschirkassin was the one who pleased me most; she is considered the greatest beauty in this country. There were besides about thirty other

after his heart. In a letter to Scheremetjeff he wrote exultingly. "God has given me and the army a recruit upon whom we may congratulate ourselves."

It is related that on the night of the Prince's birth, the Emperor sent his adjutant general to the fort to give notice of the event by the firing of guns. The soldier on guard refused admittance to the adjutant, as after the tattoo no

---

ladies, many of them are not behind our ladies in graceful and polished manners. I confess that I had not expected to find so complete and agreeable a court. The Empress has four grooms of the chamber, all handsome young gentlemen, two Russians and two Germans; the names of the Russians are Chapellof and Scheskin, and of the German Balk and Mons. The latter stands high in her favor. There are various others composing the household of the Empress, such as a steward, a master of the horse, and so forth. The pages wore green with red trimmings and gilt lace, which is also worn by the trumpeters and buglers. The lackeys and grooms of the stable, of whom there are a large number, wear no lace, but dress handsomely. The chapel is furnished with a number of German musicians who wear a handsome green uniform, although it is not usual for musicians to be dressed in livery. In a word I have found the Tzarina's court as complete and as pleasing as almost any court in Germany. That of the Tzar, however, is wretched. It consists almost entirely of a few dentschsky or inferior servants, most of whom are low-born. Nevertheless they have a good deal to say.—Journal of Bergholz in Busching's Magazine: XIX-XXII. In Russian published by Ammon, Moscow, 1863.

one must presume to enter the fort. Then the Tzar himself went and was no less positively denied admittance. "But, fellow," exclaimed the Tzar, "the Empress has given birth to a Prince."

"A Prince!" shouted the soldier. "Come in, if they shoot me dead to-morrow."

On the 17th of November, 1715, the great celebration of the baptism took place. At table there was an original entertainment. Two large pasties were brought in, one for the ladies and one for the gentlemen. Out of the first when cut, a male dwarf arose, out of the second, a female. Both made a pretty discourse, drank to the health of the Tzar, the Tzarina, the new-born Prince, and the guests, and then danced a comical dance on the table.

The little Schischetka, which was the pet name of the Prince, was cared for with the utmost solicitude. Their affection for him often appears in the letters of the Tzar and Tzarina. In the summer of 1718 the Tzarina writes: "Our dear Schischetka speaks often of his dear papa;" and a few weeks later: "Our dear Schischetka has by the help of God developed every day, and takes the greatest delight in military exercises and guns." She speaks also of his great dissatisfaction at the Tzar's absence. "I beg you to take me under your protection, I have the most terrible battles with him if I tell him you have gone away. That is something he will not tolerate. But if any one tells him papa is here, he is happy." When the first teeth appeared, the father was delighted with the news.

After Alexis was put out of the way Peter Petrovitch was announced as the Tzarevitch. His glory, however, was short lived. The year following the death of Alexis, on the 25th of April 1719, the same year in which the Tzar lost Count Scheremetjeff, one of his best generals, and the discoverer of Catharine, his hope and joy was struck down as by lightning.

Peter's grief was as unbounded as had been his delight in his son. For days and nights he remained shut up, neither eating nor drinking and seeing no one. Even the Tzarina dared not intrude upon the disconsolate father.

Gloom and silence reigned at the Court and in the capital; the news of Peter's despair and indifference to all but his grief spread in all directions. The enemies of his innovations bestirred themselves believing their hour was come. Catharine, informed of the danger, called upon the Senate with Dolgorucky at its head to come to the Tzar.,

Then Dolgorucky, who often succeeded in vanquishing the Tzar's obstinacy, said :

"Does your Majesty wish the Russians to choose for themselves another ruler? The Empire is falling into confusion, business is paralyzed, the vanquished enemy lifts up his head. Can you see all your work overthrown?"

The Tzar heeded the admonition and returned to life and activity. But he did not abandon his grief, which he carried with him to the end of his days. The son for whose sake he had offered up Alexis, fate, as if in scorn, as if in vengeance, had suddenly torn from him. Who now should carry on the work he had begun?

Peter's favorite was his daughter Anna, who very much resembled him. Some one has given this description of her: "Peter's large features are imprinted upon her face, Peter's soul shines out from her eyes, only nature and education have beautified both. Her form, slender and well proportioned, causes her uncommon height to be overlooked, and her height enhances the majesty of her appearance. But one does not recognize in her smile the soft womanliness of the Graces."

Peter was diligent in educating his daughter Anna in the art of government, believing that after his and Catharine's death she would be called to the throne. She had more intelligence, character and culture than any Russian princess of her day. Besides Russian she understood French, German, Italian and Swedish. She possessed intrepidity and presence of mind, and was—wonderful to relate—moral in the midst of the unrestrained viciousness of her times. It was a period when any one might venture to approach even persons occupying the highest position with the baldest propositions of love, and we find nothing to wonder at in the story of Count Apraxyn who, infatuated with Anna's beauty threw himself at her feet, and presenting her his sword, exclaimed :

"I love you. Listen to me, or end my torment."

The Princess took the offered sword and answered :

"I will end it."

The impassioned Count vanished in a twinkling.

Numerous suitors for the hand of the Princess presented themselves. Amongst them an ambassador arrived with propositions* from Louis XIV. But Anna was already betrothed to the Duke of Holstein. The Duke, as regards outward appearance, was little suited to the beautiful daughter of the Tzar. A contemporary sent the following report of him to Germany: " He is of medium height and well proportioned; has thick lips and a broad tongue which occasions a difficulty in his speech. While quite young, he accompanied his cousin the King of Sweden on a Polish campaign in very cold weather. Seeing the King endure the cold with such indifference he was ashamed to complain, and his toes were frozen, in consequence of which he lost several of them."

He was, however, gifted, intelligent and high-minded.

The betrothal took place in 1724 and the marriage shortly after Peter's death. The portion of the Emperor's daughter consisted, besides jewels, of 150,000 gold ducats and a yearly apanage.

The marriage was of short duration, as the Duke died on the 15th of May, 1728.

THE BRIDES OF PETER II.

The Princess Marie Mentschikoff.—The Vengeance of Eudoxia.—Mentschikoff's Fall and Banishment.—The Princess Catharine Dolgorucky.—Sudden Death of Peter II.

FATE had terribly avenged the crime committed in the death of the Tzarevitch Alexis. After the death of Catharine I., when the son of Alexis ascended the throne came the expiation.

Peter II. owed his elevation to the throne to Prince Mentschikoff—to the man who had accomplished the ruin of his grandmother and his father. It was Mentschikoff who prevailed upon Catharine to make a will leaving the succession to the Grand Duke, still in his minority.

But if Mentschikoff—Mentschikoff who was

cunning as well as cruel—advocated such a project, he had his own purpose in so doing.

The favorite seemed to have reached the highest pinnacle of human grandeur. He was a Prince of the German Empire, the Russian Duke of Ingermannland, Generalissimo of the Imperial forces, and Prime Minister. His very name carried with it a magic power, his wealth was boundless. But all this did not suffice for his ambition. He wished not only to reign silently, but to possess in addition the outward attributes of majesty.

Therefore it was that Catharine's will, made under pressure from Mentschikoff, provided not only that the little Peter Alexejevitch should ascend the throne at the death of the Tzarina, and that Mentschikoff should be Governor of the young Tzar and ruler of the Empire during his minority, but should at his majority also become his father-in-law.

Mentschikoff's daughter Empress of Russia!

Why not? Had not the low-born Catharine attained this eminence?

And Maria Alexandrovna, Mentschikoff's pretty daughter, was brilliantly educated, and under the care of an excellent mother had grown up noble and pure amid the wild passions of the day.

After the death of Catharine Peter II. ascended the throne, and a few days after, June 6, 1727, the betrothal to Maria Alexandrovna took place. The marriage was to be celebrated with the delay only of a few months. The bride received the title of Imperial Highness and her name was mentioned with the imperial family in the offices of the church. Fate seemed to have bestowed everything upon the great upstart, and to have no favor left to grant.

But the fortune of Mentschikoff was more than he was able to support, and his insolence knew no bounds. His enemies grew and grew —the envious, the malevolent and the patriots who wished to save the country from disaster. To all this, however, he paid no heed; he laughed to scorn threatenings and defied dangers.

But slowly, silently, surely, advanced the Nemesis. The house of Dolgorucky was the point where all the threads of the conspiracy against Mentschikoff centered. Young Ivan Dolgorucky was the friend of Peter's youth, and Ivan's sister Catharine was the woman whom he loved—for the young Tzar felt no inclination for his betrothed bride, Maria Alexandrovna. All the blandishments and seductions of the daughter of the man who had been his tormentor, who watched with jealousy his every step, who held him bound with heavy chains, were met by him with cold indifference. He would be no longer a child. With his thirteen years he felt himself a man and entitled to have a voice in his affairs. And Mentschikoff held him in bondage, dealt with him as he had dealt with the Tzarevitch Alexis.

And there were those who whispered in the Tzar's ear, low, but earnestly and impressively, the story of the death of the Tzarevitch and Mentschikoff's share in it. And if in such hours, when the boy was darkly brooding, his betrothed approached him, would have stroked his burning cheeks or kissed his quivering lips, he dashed her from him angrily and sought the house of Ivan Dolgorucky.

There friendship and love invited him.

Ivan's young and beautiful sister possessed the heart of Peter, which his betrothed had wooed in vain. It was here that he learned hatred and scorn of Mentschikoff and gathered courage for his final resolve to revolt and shake off his yoke, and to wring from him his consent to the recall of Eudoxia. The latter came with wild joy to foster in the heart of her grandson the thirst for vengeance which had already taken root there.

Mentschikoff's hour had struck.

A trifling fraud scarcely worthy of mention, of far less importance than many of which he had been guilty, was made the occasion of his fall. A sentence of terrible severity was passed upon him. From the summit of his power he and with him his whole family sunk into the deepest depths of misery and degradation.

From his palace on the Neva, the most splendid in the capital, which ten years before had been the scene of the most important festivities, from his flaunting palace, Mentschikoff went forth to the dangers and desolation of Siberian exile. His hapless daughter, yesterday honored as an Empress, walked brokenhearted by the side of her grief-stricken mother and her despairing brother. While the father endured with proud courage his terrible misfortune, Maria Alexandrovna, who loved Peter and could not comprehend the catastrophe, pined, and sickened, and died, before she reached her destined place of banishment.

Into Mentschikoff's place stepped young Ivan Dolgorucky, into Maria Alexandrovna's the Princess Catharine. The marriage was arranged to take place in a few months. The bride received the title of Imperial Highness and her name was united to the imperial family in the church offices. But before the ceremony took place the young Tzar fell ill of the small-pox and died suddenly.

THE EMPRESS ANNA AND BIRON.

Anna's marriage with the Duke of Courland.—His early death. — Anna's favorite, Bühren-Biron.— Biron's wife.—Biron's end.

THE first princess of the house of Romanoff who married a German prince was the niece of Peter the Great, Anna Ivanovna. Her marriage with the Duke of Courland was celebrated in St. Petersburg. Russian custom required that two days before the wedding two of the Tzar's chamberlains should go from palace to palace in a gala coach and invite to the ceremony the home and foreign ministers and other persons of importance on both sides of the Neva.

On this occasion the Tzar himself performed the part of grand marshal. He wore a red cloak trimmed with sable, a silver sword, the order of Saint Andrew attached to a blue ribbon, a white perruque, and carried in his hand as a token of his office a large baton bedecked with gay and costly ribbons.

The wedding, like all the great festivities of the time, was celebrated in the palace of Prince Mentschikoff, where a chapel had been erected in one of the apartments. Upon a small altar was placed a silver-mounted bible and near it a burning light, a small silver chest which contained the Russian *Bog* or "God," and the two prince's coronets, which are held over the heads of the bride and groom during the ceremony. During the repast wreaths of laurel were suspended over the heads of the bride, bridegroom and princesses. Those over the heads of the newly wedded pair were torn down the next day, while those over the heads of the unmarried princesses according to the requirement, were left intact.

The closing feature of the marriage consisted of fireworks showing the names of the bridal pair, and a picture representing Cupid smelting two hearts together in a furnace, with the Russian inscription below: "Out of two I make one."

The Duke's connubial bliss lasted just fourteen days. He died suddenly on his return journey from Courland.

The Duchess mourned the loss of her husband

but soon found consolation in her valet, Ernst Johann Bühren.

Bühren's grandfather had been, in the middle of the seventeenth century, groom of the stables to James, third duke of Courland. The son of the stable boy, Charles, rose to be duke's forester, which enabled him to educate his three sons, Charles, Ernst Johann and Gustav, for a higher station.

Ernst Johann was born on the 12th of November, 1690. He studied at Königsberg and it is said he once made an effort to obtain the position of groom of the chamber to the Tzarevitch Alexis but met with a rebuff on account of his low birth.

He was more successful at Mitau, where in 1720 he became groom of the chamber to the widowed Duchess Anna of Courland, winning the favor of his mistress to such a degree that she gave him the situation of—her late husband.

Anna was far from beautiful. Her nose was of extraordinary length and her face marked with the smallpox. Her step was halting, and she waddled like a duck. Biron's face possessed not a single attractive feature, his manners were rude and coarse, and it must have been the influence of his robust and powerful physique upon Anna's sensual nature, that gave him such an ascendency over her that to the end of her life she never revolted against his brutal despotism. She respected the external forms of propriety by marrying him to a Miss Benigen Gottliebe of Trotha or Treyden, who acted the part of mother to her child.

Bühren meanwhile relinquished his name of Bühren for the more aristocratic sounding one of Biron and sought admittance among the nobility of Courland, but in spite of Anna's protection he was bluntly refused. He established himself with his household, in the palace of his paramour, which, as the Duchess's valet, he could appropriately do without disregarding appearances. The meals were taken together in Biron's apartments.

After the death of Peter the Second, Anna was called to occupy the Russian throne, but not without having first consented to ratify a constitution, and having given a promise that her favorite, Biron, whose fame had outrun the limits of Courland, should not be permitted to enter Russia.

Both of these promises were broken.

She was no sooner established on the throne than Biron was summoned to her side, and the whole powers of the government were entrusted into his hands, nothing more being heard of a constitution.

Instead of deposing the faithless Empress and her paramour, both people and magnates, as is characteristic of Russia, bowed their heads low before the upstart. Biron received the rank of Count, and was made knight successively of all the highest orders of Russia. It was not long before foreign nations became aware of the new ruler of Russia, and all the courts of Europe hastened to do him homage. The Emperor Charles made him a Count of the Empire, and the King of Poland conferred upon him the order of the White Eagle.

The distinctions lavished upon Biron attracted the attention of the French Duke de Biron to his powerful namesake in Russia. He wrote inquiring with courteously veiled irony whether he had the honor of being related to him. The Lord Bühren-Biron was shrewd enough to reply to this letter with silence, answering derision with disdain. He had his consolations. His consequence, power and riches increased daily, and it was not long before he had the splendid satisfaction of succeeding to the last duke of Courland, of being placed at the head of the proud nobility who had disdainfully rejected his petition to become one of their number. The satirical Duke de Biron—this time seriously—sent an ambassador to his illustrious kinsman congratulating him upon his accession to the throne.

Duke Bühren-Biron, like all parvenus, was fond of pomp and ostentation, and this was reason sufficient to cause the most lavish expenditure at the Russian Court. The memoirs and histories of the period are filled with accounts of the prodigality of the Russian Court, which is described as the most magnificent in the world.*

All this, however, was external merely and underneath there was barbarian rudeness

---

* Weber, Das veränderte Russland, 1738–1740. History and Deeds of the Empress Anna, St. Petersburg, 1741. Schmidt-Phiseldeck, Hermaa, Leipzig, 1786. G. A. W. von Helbig, Russisch Günstlinge, Tübingen, 1809. Crusenstolpe, Der Russische Hof., Hamburg, 1855. Ssolowjeff, History of Russia. Vol. XIX. Mémoires du duc de Liria, Paris, 1788. Russian: St. Petersburg, 1840. History of the Election and Accession to the Throne of the Empress Anna Ivanovna. In the Moscow Westink, 1830. Manstein, Mémoires Historiques, Politiques et Militaires sur la Russie, Depuis, 1727-1744. Avec la Vie de l'auteur par Hüber, Leipzig, 1771. Memoirès of the Princess Natalia Borissofna Dolgorucky. In the "Friend of Youth," Year 1810, No. 1, Russian. The same memoirs are also contained in the Biography of the Dolgorucky family, St. Petersburg, 1842, pp. 128-156, also in the Russian Archives, 1867. I.

and lack of taste. "It is to no purpose," observes a chronicler, "that they bedeck themselves in cloth of silver and gold, when with the costly garments they wear the most wretchedly curled perruques, or the most beautiful stuffs botched by the hand of an unskilful tailor. A richly dressed man rides in a wretched coach drawn by sorry jades. For one well dressed person ten may be seen dressed in the most miserable taste. The physique of the women is generally good; one sees many pretty faces, but few handsome forms."

There was the same want of harmony in the appointments of the houses. In the most luxurious apartments the dirt was as thick as one's finger in the corners and on the walls. Gold poured from Russia into foreign countries, there being as yet no manufactories of luxuries in Russia. The large number of court balls may be imagined when it is stated that every person who could in any degree be reckoned among the number of the court nobles was compelled to expend from two to three thousand rubles for clothing annually—three thousand rubles, at a time when the proudest palaces in the capital cost only twelve thousand!

Notwithstanding his relations with the Empress, Biron made a distinguished marriage. His Duchess understood her advantage. She loved indolence and display; her diamonds were worth two millions, and her magnificent equipage was drawn by the most costly horses in the whole country. All this luxury of Madame Biron's was paid for by the Duke's paramour, or rather by the Russian people, who for ten long years had been drained in the most unexampled manner by the parvenu. Famine reigned far and near, whole towns fell into decay, parents killed their children to save them from the misery and starvation into which excessive contributions had plunged the whole population.

Is it a wonder that the tormented people at length revolted and endeavored to expel the usurper, the "Monster Biron," from the land? Unhappily, the revolution was betrayed and stifled in its germ. Its only result was to furnish the ruthless destroyer occasion to carry on with increased vigor the business of executioner. The Tzarina offered no resistance. She was so completely in Biron's power that he dared to strike her when she presumed to intercede for those whom he had condemned.

When the Empress was nearing the end of her days, Biron, like his successor and prototype Mentschikoff, formed projects for securing the throne to himself. He persuaded Anna to choose as her successor her nephew Joan Antonovitch of Brunswick, an infant in the arms, with himself as regent during the minority.

But as with Mentschikoff so was it with Biron.

The regency was numbered by weeks. The people gathered courage, and one night Biron and his family were taken from their warm and sumptuous beds and carried off to prison.

After Biron's person had been secured, the confiscation of his effects began. The value of the treasures found in his palace amounted to fourteen millions of rubles. Amongst them was a toilet of pure gold studded with precious stones of great price. In Mitau, Libau and Windau, all the Duke's effects were placed under seal. In May 1741 the judgment pronounced against the former Duke Regent was published. It was death. But the Regent Anna who governed in the name of her infant son, commuted the sentence to perpetual banishment and imprisonment at Pelim, in Siberia. In this miserable hamlet of sixty houses, 600 versts in the rear of Tobolsk, the fallen parvenu occupied a little hut of which his arch rival, Münnich, had himself laid the foundation. When Elizabeth a short while after ascended the throne, she recalled Biron from banishment. As the exile was returning home he met on the way his enemy Münnich, who, banished by Elizabeth, was on his way to Pelim to occupy the hut which he had built for Biron and muse on the transitoriness of Russian greatness.

Biron went to Jaroslaw, and lived there with his family a retired and tranquil life until the end of Elizabeth's reign. Peter the Third recalled him to the court. He came, and threw himself gratefully at the monarch's feet. Münnich also soon made his appearance at Peter's court. Peter began his reign with the recall of the exiles, a generous but imprudent measure. When Biron and Münnich met for the first time at the court, the Tzar exclaimed: "Ah, here are two good old friends, they must drink together." Biron and Münnich glowered darkly at each other as they replaced the glasses on the table and turned away.

The accession of Catharine was for Biron a happy event, for she reinstated him as Duke of Courland (1763). The judgments passed upon his last reign have been contradictory. According to some it was no less severe than before; according to others Biron became in his old age a loyal and even generous ruler. He died in 1772 at the age of eighty-two, and the Court of Russia wore mourning for him for eight days.

Biron left two sons and a daughter. His son Peter, born in 1724, had imperial blood in his veins and bore a strong resemblance to Anna. In the last ten years of Biron's life he exercised the sovereignty in Courland and his government was a stormy one, his rapacity having made him thoroughy detested. Finally the Courlanders appealed to Catharine to deliver them from the Duke (1795). Catharine evinced the most generous alacrity in coming to the aid of the unhappy Courlanders. She deposed Peter from the sovereignty and thrust it into her own pocket, into which she had already thrust portions of Turkey and Poland.

Peter was thrice married: to a Princess Waldeck, a Princess Jussupoff, and the Countess Anna Charlotte Dorothea Medum. The first two wives hated him and abandoned him outright. With the last he lived happily enough for a time, but the marriage at length became one of misery, and it was a happy event for the poor Countess when in 1800 the ex-Duke died.

Anna Charlotte and Dorothea, the sister of the celebrated authoress, Elise von der Recke, and herself a woman of intellect, with an ardent love of the beautiful, had by Peter four daughters. The oldest, Catharine Frederika, married Prince Rohan, separated from him and married Trubetskoy, from whom she was also separated. On her estates she was known as the Duchess of Segan. The second daughter of Charlotte Dorothea, Maria Paulina, married the hereditary Prince of Hohenzollern-Hechingen, but lived apart from her husband; the third, Johanna Catharine, married the Duke of Acerenza Belmonte-Pignatelli and separated from him; the fourth followed the example of her sisters.

The daughter of Duke Ernest Johann Biron, Hedwig Elizabeth, born in 1727, had already suitors in 1740; amongst them the father of the appanaged Prince of Sachsen-Meiningen asked for her in marriage. But the Duke being then in the zenith of his power the appanaged Prince of Sachsen-Meiningen was too humble an alliance, and the suitor was bluntly dismissed. Biron's fall ensued not long after and his daughter would have remained a spinster had not in 1759, a simple lieutenant, Baron Tscherkasson decided to marry her. This marriage, also, like all the marriages in the Biron family, was unhappy.

THE EMPRESS ELIZABETH AND HER LOVERS.

Elizabeth's Betrothed.—Her First Lover, the Soldier Schubin.—His Banishment to Siberia.—The Singer Rasumovsky, the Husband of an Empress.—Michael Woronsoff.—Streetsweepers, Coachmen, Servants and Hostlers, the Empress's Lovers.—The Two Schuvalovs.—The Rejected Empress.—Elizabeth's Children.—Character of the Tzarina Elizabeth, the Good.

ASTONISHING! That the same century whose early years saw the women of Russia languishing in the deepest depths of oriental seclusion, saw also the imperial throne almost exclusively occupied by women. Not one of them, however, showed herself worthy of the great task which suddenly devolved upon her. All of them suffered the Empire to be governed by favorites of the lowest class.

To Catharine I. succeeded, after the short interregnum of Peter II., Anna Ivanovna, who, after the few weeks' "reign" of the infant son of Ivan Antonovitch was succeeded in the year 1740 by Elizabeth, the daughter of Peter the Great. Unlike her sister Anna the favorite of Peter, who died early, Elizabeth was from her earliest youth lost to all sense of shame. She was the worst of all the Russian Messalinas,* worse than Catharine I., or even than Catharine II. Catharine I. contented herself with a few lovers, Anna Ivanovna with but one. Catharine II. was a woman of gifted intellect who conferred many benefits upon the Empire and who externally at least might be deemed to possess a claim to her surname of Great. Elizabeth possessed not a single attribute of a

---

* Chronique Scandaleuse des Petersburger Hofes seit den Zeiten der Kaiserin Elisabeth, Fürth, 1832. F. L. A. Horschelmann, Pragmatische Geschichte der Merkwürdigsten Staats-veränderungen im Russischen Reiche, von dem Ableben Peters des Grossen, bis Katharina II., Erfurt, 1763. Lacombe, Histoire des Révolutions de l'Empire de Russie, Amsterdam, 1778. Pekarsky, the Marquis de la Chetardie in Russia, St. Petersburg, 1862. Graf zu Lynar, Hinterlassene Staatsschriften, 2 Bände, Hamburg, 1793-1797. Compare with this: Jansen, Rochus Friedrich Graff zu Lynar, Oldenburg, 1873. Friedrichs des Grossen Nachgelassene Schriften III., IV., V. Wassiltschikoff, The Rasumovsky Family, St. Petersburg, 1880. Ernst Herrmann, Der Russische Hof unter Kaiserin Elisabeth. Historisches Taschenbuch,

sovereign. She had neither the ability nor the disposition to govern her powerful Empire; she was as incapable as she was corrupt, as drunken as she was dissolute. The disorderly life which she led enervated not only her body but her mind, which nature had not highly endowed. She showed an ever-increasing apathy in regard to everything except sensual excitements, which alone could dispel her torpor. She was deficient in every kind of education, for her understanding of German and French as well as Russian could not be reckoned as education. Neither had she any comprehension of politics. She was friendly toward France because the French Minister, the Marquis de la Chetardie, had won her favor and been instrumental in her elevation to the

---

VI., I., Leipzig, 1882. Schäfer, Aus den Letzten Tagen der Kaiserin Elisabeth von Russland, Historische Zeitschrift XXXVI. Hanway, Beschreibung der Reise von London durch Russland und Persien, Hamburg, 1754. Correspondence of Ivan Ivanovitch Schuvaloff, Russian Archives, 1864, 4; 1869, 11; 1870, 8, 9. Michael Illarianowitch Woronzoff, Archives of Prince Woronzoff, Moscow, 1870, 1871, 1892, and Russian Archives, 1870, 8 and 9. Schtcherbatoff, Corruption of Morals in Russia, edited in London. Compare Semewsky, Russkaja Starina, 1870, 7 and 8; Galachoff's Historische Chrestomathie, Vol. I. Schlosser, Geschischte des Achtzehnten Jahrhunderts. Also the works on Peter III. and Catharine II.

throne; she was friendly to Austria and Saxony because these powers were subservient to herself, but the great Frederick who made her the target for his wit, she abhorred.

During weeks and months she held herself completely aloof from affairs of State. If she gave them a thought it was with the utmost listlessness, and at times was not even to be persuaded to affix her name to important State papers. The answer to a letter from Louis XV. announcing the birth of a grandson, was held back for three years because Elizabeth was too much occupied with her love affairs to sign it. In a conversation with her nephew the day before her death, she is said to have exacted from him a promise that no harm should befall her favorites, especially Kirill Rasumovsky and Ivan Schuvaloff, but not a word as to her duties as sovereign.

Elizabeth received the surname of "the Good" on account of a promise which she made upon her accession not to inflict the death penalty. Banishment to Siberia and the knout came only the more into prominence. More than eighty thousand persons—often for the most trifling offences, or upon the merest suspicion—more than eighty thousand persons were knouted, mutilated, banished, during

Elizabeth's reign. For all these the death penalty would have been a benevolent infliction. In comparison with the sufferings which the exiles of that day endured, Kennan's descriptions of the Siberia of to-day are pictures of light; for Elizabeth, who had herself come to the throne by a revolution, was in perpetual fear of being violently deposed.

In appearance the Empress bore a strong resemblance to her mother. According to the report of those who knew her, while she might have been more delicately modeled, her figure was on the whole extremely graceful. " Her air and step were majestic, her skin remarkably fine, her eyes bright and her glance captivating. Her accent and manner of speaking were gracious and pleasing." She had chestnut brown hair, and dark brows which enhanced the beauty of her large blue eyes, a peculiarly attractive smile, that easily changed to a jovial laugh showing a row of white teeth. She was always cordial to her friends and affable to those about her. Gay, amiable, animated, the Tzarina Elizabeth produced the most charming impression upon men.

The Duke de Lyria, the Spanish Ambassador, who was very unfriendly to her and lost no opportunity of descanting upon her vices, could not but admit that she was a woman of extraordinary beauty. Not only men such as the French Ministers, La Vie and Campredon, went into raptures over her beauty, even women were forced to recognize and admit that she was beautiful.

Her hand had been early sought in marriage. When a child her sister Anna had formed a project of marrying her to Louis XV., then to the Duke de Chartres, Condé, and to the Duke de Biron. As she grew up the Germans followed the French—Prince August Bischoff von Lubec, Duke Ferdinand of Courland, Prince Maurice of Saxony, Prince Frederick of Sulzbach, the Margrave Charles of Brandenburg-Baireuth and Prince Peter Biron. Even the Infanta of Portugal, Dom Manuel, and the son of the Shah, asked for her hand. In Russia there was naturally no lack of adorers; the young Tzar Peter II. was in love with his aunt, Dolgorucky also, the Tzar's friend, and young Prince Mentschikoff. Before the death of Catharine I. Elizabeth was finally betrothed to the Duke of Holstein-Eutin, who died on the very day set for the marriage. She seems to have been greatly attached to him and to have mourned his loss. Even long years after and in the period of her greatest immorality, she kept the anniversary of his death in pious remembrance. Her distress at his loss was such that she resolved never to marry at all. This resolution she adhered to in so far that she never really gave her hand officially to any of her numerous wooers, but she lavished the most ardent affection upon her lovers, and soon ceased to be ashamed of actions at which the most immodest might blush.

With her first favorite, the soldier Schubin, she withdrew to a suburb of the capital, and to avoid recognition they frequented together the country and forests, where, however, the two supposed men were now and then unseasonably surprised.

During the lifetime of Catharine, and even under Peter II., this affair remained to some extent a secret, but under the Tzarina Anna it became notorious and scandalous, and when Schubin went so far as to insult the Grand Duchess before the whole Court, the Empress saw herself constrained to banish her cousin's lover to Siberia, where he remained many years.

Elizabeth was inconsolable, and in the despair of her heart, instead of grieving to death over the lover of whom she had been robbed, she took several.

One of the most prominent of her next lovers was Alexis Rasumovsky, the son of a peasant of Ukraine, whose fine voice obtained for him the position of Imperial singer and who in this capacity won her approval. After Schubin's banishment, the Grand Duchess sent her friend Madam Ivan Ismailoff to Rasumovsky as the bearer of her offer of love, which was promptly accepted. Rasumovsky obtained the position of singer and lute player to the Grand Duchess, and was soon advanced to the dignity of superintendent of her household and lord of her heart.

The Tzarina, who had a respect for appearances, wished to banish Rasumovsky as she had banished Schubin, but this time she encountered so vigorous an opposition on the part of her cousin that she ended by permitting her to do as she pleased. When Elizabeth came to the throne * her first care was to reward her lovers.

---

*After the French Minister, the Marquis de la Chetardie, who contributed French gold to the cause and himself possessed her personal favor, Elizabeth was chiefly indebted for her throne to Johann Hermann l'Estocq, her physician, who had come to St. Petersburg a young man in 1713, and had quickly won the favor of Peter. In 1725 Catharine I. appointed him surgeon to her daughter Elizabeth, a position which he held until 1748. After the death of Peter II., l'Estocq wished to assist

Rasumofsky was made a count and brought into the palace where to the end of his life he occupied an apartment adjoining that of the Empress. But finally, as Elizabeth was no less pious than she was immoral, she suffered herself to be persuaded that her relations with him offended heaven, and to propitiate heaven

---

Elizabeth to gain the throne, but the indolent and timid princess declined his proposals. It was not till eleven years after, that she interested herself to the extent of not contradicting L'Estocq's designs, when together with Michael Woronzoff, a musician, and Schwarz-Grünstein, a soldier of the guard, the project was undertaken by which in 1741 the infant Ivan Antonovitch was deposed and the daughter of Peter the Great ascended the throne. In the beginning Elizabeth showed herself grateful to l'Estocq, and conferred upon him honors and dignities. But she soon abandoned him and permitted envious persons to bring false accusations against him on account of which he was banished to Asia. It may have contributed to l'Estocq's misfortune that his ugly wife had won the favor of the handsome Kurt von Schönberg which Elizabeth had wooed in vain. (See page 160).

Grünstein was promoted from the rank of a common soldier to be adjutant-general to the Empress and soon after to major-general. But he had the presumption to criticise her immorality and was banished to Siberia. The musician Schwarz might have enjoyed in peace the landed estate he had received from Elizabeth as the price of his deed, but a peasant girl whom he pursued and persecuted killed her master and tormentor with a pitchfork. Unclouded prosperity was enjoyed only by Michael Woronzoff, of whom we shall hear later.

a priestly marriage ceremony was secretly performed, in accordance with all the forms of consecrated unions.

The Empress was no sooner eternally bound to her lover than she wanted to be eternally rid of him. But she was two weak to dissolve the marriage, too weak even to banish her obnoxious husband from the court or the palace. He remained therefore at the side of the Empress while others performed his duties.

Soon after her accession Elizabeth bethought her of Schubin, and sent a courier to Siberia in quest of the exile. After a pursuit of years, the messenger discovered the object of his search and brought him in 1743 to St. Petersburg. But the once handsome and vigorous Schubin was now miserable and sickly. He no longer pleased the Empress. She therefore promoted him from sergeant to lieutenant general, and conferred upon him a pension and a handsome estate—at the remotest distance from St. Petersburg. There he went, and remained until his blessed end.

Schubin's place was filled by a soldier of the guard named Buturlin. Elizabeth's lovers were with one exception chosen from the lowest of the low, and her sensuality grew so refined that only the most repulsive ugliness possessed a charm for her. She was wildly infatuated with the ugliest man at the capital, a rough and dirty Kalmuck.

"Her court," says the sober Schlosser, "was composed of the rabble in the lowest sense of the term." It swarmed with persons of the commonest sort, utterly devoid of intelligence or heart, for the most part the merest outcasts, who had once enjoyed her highest favor and had filled the principal functions in the State, had received the first orders and boundless wealth.

A certain Carl Sievers, a servant of the Tzarina's who often came into her presence attracted her attention and won her regard to such an extent that she could not separate from him even while others were the recipients of her favors. He filled two offices, that of ardent lover and that of coffee-maker. Elizabeth loved coffee as much as she loved men. As Sievers discharged well both of these functions, he was rewarded with riches and honors, and, like all the rest, raised to the rank of count.

The career of Michael Woronzoff was brilliant. He rose from the lowest ranks of the people to the dignity of count and lord chancellor, and when Elizabeth tired of him she married him to her cousin, the Countess of Skavronska.

Once when the Tzarina was on a journey, she remarked a street-sweep, whose name was Ljallin, and ordered him to the palace, where he was forthwith instated as servant and lover to the Empress. Growing tired of him in a few weeks, she made him a chamberlain, a count, and the owner of a landed estate,—at a distance from St. Petersburg.

Jermolay Skvarzoff, Woshinsky, Poltarazky, were placed at the court as servants, coachmen and singers, and all three suddenly became chamberlains, counts, and finally landed proprietors; Poltarsky was made in addition director of the imperial chapel, which office he held until his death in 1795.

After Rasumovsky, the one of Elizabeth's lovers who preserved her favor the longest was Ivan Schuvaloff, a descendent of an old and noble family, at that time impoverished. Ivan was made first page, then chamberlain, and in his fiftieth year lord of the bedchamber to the Empress. He retained Elizabeth's favor until her death. He refused the Tzarina's offer of the title of count, and also the riches which she would have conferred upon him. He was modest and honorable. On her deathbed Elizabeth gave him the key of a casket which contained inestimable treasures in jewels, gold and valuable papers, and said: "All this is yours."

Schuvaloff took nothing, but gave the key to Peter the Third, the heir to the throne.

This modesty was the cause of Elizabeth's unshaken constancy. Ivan Schuvaloff never importuned her, never asked favors, was never jealous.

All the more jealous was she.

At one time she believed she had real grounds for her jealousy, but being unable to learn with exactness which of the court ladies had presumed to win even the most passing favor of Schuvaloff, the most horrible persecution of all the women and girls whom the Tzarina regarded in the light of "suspects" was instituted. They were seized and without trial subjected to the most cruel punishments. After having their heads shaved as a mark of dishonor they were thrown into houses of correction to become the prey of bandits. Whether the guilty one was actually amongst those who were thus tortured is a point concerning which history is silent.

Ivan Schuvaloff preserved, nevertheless, Elizabeth's favor. He survived her many years, passed for a jovial gentleman, was a patron of the arts and sciences, and founded the St. Petersburg Academy of Art. In the reign of Peter the Third he was prosperous, but under Catharine he met with disaster. After losing his very large fortune at play he was reduced to live on a pension of four thousand rubles. He was ninety years old when he died.

The brothers Alexander and Peter Schuvaloff enjoyed, as well as their brother Ivan, the favor of the Empress. Both of them were rapacious and cruel. Alexander was a person of little merit, but Peter possessed some reputation as a soldier and statesman. The progenitor of many distinguished Russian houses is reputed to have been the child of Elizabeth. It is tolerably certain that she had a son by Count Sakrevsky and by Rasumovsky and a daughter, the Countess Elizabeth Tarakanof, by Schuvaloff.*

---

*Helbig, "Russische Günstlinge," page 172: "Schuvaloff is said to be the father of a daughter born to Elizabeth about the year 1753. She was called Elizabeth and afterwards received, if we do not mistake, the name of Princess Tarakanof. This child for whom an Italian chambermaid of the Empress took the place of mother, was sent to Italy and grew up there. As long as the Empress lived she wanted for nothing, but after her death she was left in destitution. Schuvaloff visited Italy and saw his daughter, but without daring to make

The Tzarina's advances were not always well received. At her Court was a Saxon, Kurt von Schönberg, whom Frederick Augustus the Second had sent to Russia to organize some mining enterprises. He found the court of Elizabeth and the loose morals which prevailed there so much to his taste that he decided to remain. He was a handsome man and much sought after by the fair. Elizabeth approached him with the most unmistakable overtures, but was

himself known to her. In her seventieth year she was living there in very indigent circumstances." Archenholz in his book, "England und Italien," says: "A remarkable event occurred in Leghorn in March, 1775. A Russian lady of lowly birth but of illustrious descent, has been living for two years in Rome in the greatest poverty. Under such circumstances the idea of raising her eyes to a throne could easily germinate. She was intelligent, educated and of a gentle disposition. Her retirement was suddenly broken in upon by a Russian officer who made to her by word of mouth some startling revelations, accompanying them by a considerable present of money—an argument which in her needy circumstances had the anticipated effect. The lady suffered herself to be persuaded, and in the year.1775 she came to Pisa where Count Alexis Orloff then was. The latter received her like a queen, accompanied her everywhere, and at the theatre showed her a deference in public which astonished the whole nobility and caused every one to wonder who the lady could be toward whom the haughty Count was so obsequious. At Leghorn they were hospitably entertained by the English Consul Dyck. At the table the

respectfully repulsed. For Herr von Schönberg was already disposed of in favor of the wife of the Doctor l'Estocq to whom Elizabeth was indebted for her throne. This Madam l'Estocq, a German of humble birth by the name of Miller, was ugly, drunken and dirty. Nevertheless she was preferred by the handsome Kurt to a munificent and beautiful Empress. Who can fathom the heart of man! The older Elizabeth grew the more inordinate grew her vanity, her love of display and

conversation fell on the fleet, and the lady not having been on board of a man of war consented to visit one of the vessels. Little dreaming what awaited her she got into a boat with the Count, and on reaching the vessel was lifted in. Here at once the scene changed. She was handcuffed and disdainfully informed that she was a prisoner. The ship remained two days longer at the port making preparations for her voyage to Russia. Meanwhile, no strange ship was allowed to approach her. On the third day she set sail with her booty. The court expressed its displeasure very distinctly over this procedure and the whole city was aroused over the event." So much for Archenholz. Helbig continues: "The lady was taken to St. Petersburg. There she was accused of being insane and confined first in the fortress and afterwards at Schlüsselberg where in 1776 she expired, not without suspicion of a violent death." In addition to this narrative of Helbig's see the section "Eine Prätendentin" in Brückner's classic work upon Catharine the Second, Berlin, 1883, pp. 208-217. On this subject Brückner also in 1891, presented some interesting new developments in the *Muncher Neuesten Nachrichten* under the

her jealousy of beautiful women. It was a peculiarity of hers to wear every day a different costume. She was careful and cleanly, and her style of dress was tasteful, sumptuous and extravagant. She thought to enhance her beauty by appearing always differently gowned, changing her attire a half dozen if not a dozen times a day, and seldom wearing the same gown more than once. Her most magnificent toilet was in the afternoon upon rising from her midday siesta at which she usually had

---

title: " Ein rätselhafter Todesfall im Hause der Romanows." Brückner does not accept Helbig's statement, and says: " The real facts of the case show us that Catharine acted in this affair, not from purely personal considerations, but out of regard for the safety of her Empire, energetically, firmly and resolutely, to meet a danger whose consequences in a period which had brought forth a Pugatschef, it was difficult to foresee." He characterizes the story related of the Countess Tarakanof as sensational and devoid of any historical basis. According to him, the lady, who did not bear the name of Tarakanof and was not the daughter of Schuvaloff, but of Kirill (not Alexis) Rasumovsky, was a mere adventuress and sharper who made pretentions to the throne and was repudiated. Melnikow, "the Princess Tarakanof and the Princess von Wladimir," St. Petersburg, 1888, has assembled all the data with regard to Elizabeth's supposed children. See, lastly, W. Panin, Papers of the Historical and Antiquarian Society of Moscow, 1867, I., and the German work: Die vorgebliche Töchter der Kaiserin Elisabeth. Berlin, 1867. Von G. B. (Brevern).

the company of one of her favorites. Among her effects after her death were found more than fifteen thousand perfectly new gowns, two large chests full of silk stockings, two of silk ribbons, thousands of shoes and slippers, and huge piles of costly stuffs. The greater part of the fifteen thousand gowns were in the form of wrappers, as the Empress usually went to bed intoxicated and could not easily be undressed. They were therefore made very simply so as to admit of being easily ripped off. When at the celebration of the conclusion of peace with Turkey the play "Oleg," in which seven hundred persons took part, was produced by Catharine II. at the St. Petersburg theatre, the women's costumes were drawn from the wardrobe of Elizabeth, and such magnificent toilettes were never seen upon a stage at one time.

Elizabeth's envy kept pace with her vanity. No woman of her Court must be esteemed beautiful by comparison with herself. Unfortunately, there was a Madam Lapuchin whose beauty even the Empress herself could not disavow, and who became the object of her most violent rage and hatred. At last an opportunity arose to gratify her vengeance. Being informed that Madame Lapuchin had spoken evil of herself, she caused her to be arrested and knouted. The punishment was inflicted in the presence of the Tzarina, who had inherited her father's taste for witnessing executions. An eye witness has described the terrible scene.* One of the jailers tore off a sort of cloak which concealed the bosom of the beautiful Lapuchin. The condemned woman shrank back with offended modesty, turned pale and sobbed. She was seized by rude hands and in a moment her clothing was torn off, leaving her exposed naked to her girdle to the eager gaze of an enormous crowd.

She was then taken by an executioner and bound to the back of another, while with a knout especially prepared for her she was whipped until the flesh hung from her in ribbons. At last the poor woman was taken almost lifeless, placed in a wretched vehicle and transported to Siberia.

This was the last great deed of the Tzarina Elizabeth, whom Russian historians have named " the Good."

---

*Voyage en Sibérie par M. l'Abbé Chappe d'Auteroche. Amsterdam, 1770, II. 368, in which will be found a description of this scene.

MARRIAGE AND AMOURS OF PETER THE FOOLISH.

Peter's Character.—His Education.—Catharine, Born Princess of Zerbst.—Peter's Excesses.—Elizabeth Romanovna Woronzoff.—Catharine's craftiness.—Princess Dashkoff.—The End of Peter and Elizabeth Voronzoff.

PETER THE THIRD, the most pitiable Tzar who ever occupied the throne of the Romanoffs, was a strange admixture of good intentions and follies. He became early penetrated with a horror of servitude, a love of equality and an enthusiasm for heroic deeds. But he could love what was good only in a petty fashion, and when he would fain have imitated his prototypes, he learned only their idiosyncracies. Peter the Great having risen from the rank of pikeman, Peter the Third wished to enter the army as a private soldier; and because he idolized Frederick the Second, he wore like him narrow gamashes and dressed his body guard in the Prussian uniform.*

Upon ascending the throne Peter recalled the administrative exiles, a generous act, whose consequences, however, were evil. The Empire, the city, and the Court were soon filled with persons seeking vengeance for their wrongs. At the Court especially, the most determined and bitter enemies such as Biron, Münnich and l'Estocq, encountered each other. Peter, in his relations with them, showed the most mischievous lack of address.

He thought he could best exhibit his contempt for everything Russian by showing his partiality for what was German, or Prussian, and he thereby drew upon himself the bitter hatred of those whom he wished to control.

---

*Peter the Third inherited military tastes from his father, Charles Frederick. The Duke made his son a common soldier when a mere child, afterwards promoting him to the rank of a subaltern officer. On a birthday the little Prince was required to mount guard in the dining room, being relieved during the repast in regular fashion, and promoted to lieutenant for his soldierly bearing. From this time on Peter's constant association was with officers, and from this time dates his fondness for a military life, a fondness which degenerated into the ridiculous, and contributed largely to his downfall and melancholy end. In spite of his soldierly proclivities, Peter was all his life the veriest coward.

And there were enough in the land to whom the grandson of Peter the Great was an object of abhorrence. That he had thus developed was the natural consequence of the atmosphere in which he had been reared.

Peter was born at Kiel, on the 10th of February, 1728 (old style). He was given the name of Karl Peter Ulrich, after his father, his maternal grandfather and his father's aunt. His career began inauspiciously. During the festivities attending the celebration of his baptism a chest of powder exploded. A short while after, his mother caught a cold of which she died. Peter was then not three years old. The widowed Duke of twenty-eight years had not even during the lifetime of his wife been distinguished for his domestic virtues. The Duchess often complained of him to her sister, the Grand Duchess Elizabeth: "The Duke and Mavruschka (Mavra Jogorovna Schepelof, the Duke's mistress) are quite disreputable. He is never at home, and they drive or attend the theatre together."

He now neglected his home altogether. Until the year 1735 the education of Prince Charles Peter was left entirely to women. In his seventh year he was placed in charge of members of the Holstein nobility. With the exception of the French language which he learned in his earliest childhood from the women by whom he was surrounded and for the study of which hours were still set apart, the only thing he learned was Latin. At last, when it began to appear probable that he would succeed to the throne of Russia, he received instruction in the Russian language and religion. It does not appear, however, that his instruction was such as was likely to inspire him with any love of them.

Peter was eleven years old when in the summer of 1739 his father died leaving his son only a heavily burdened dukedom. He came under the guardianship of the Bishop of Lubeck, Adolph Friedrich, afterwards King of Sweden, a relative of the Prince on his father's side, by which his opportunities for an education were in no wise bettered. The tutors to whom he was confided were two men who instead of forming the character of their pupil, destroyed it. One of them, von Brümmer, was a low intriguer and profligate, a good horseman, but utterly unfitted to be tutor to a prince. He was also unfriendly to his pupil, quarreled with him incessantly, and was roughly abusive for the smallest offence. The other, Bergholz,* gave himself no concern whatever for his charge, leaving him entirely in the hands of Brümmer.

Notwithstanding that Prince Charles Peter Ulrich was a weak and sickly child, Brümmer often suffered him to go without food from early in the morning until two o'clock. If he surreptitiously procured dry bread and ate until he had appeased his hunger, and Brümmer remarked at table his want of appetite, he sent him to stand in a corner and look on while the others ate. There was no lack even of heavy blows, and other measures appropriate to impress on the child a sense of his own dignity. In return, the latter showed himself passionate and wilful. Peter was all his life a braggadocio, a peculiarity which afterwards caused him to be much ridiculed in St. Petersburg where he was known to be a great coward.

A sudden project was set on foot to place the young Prince not on the Russian but on the Swedish throne, and instruction in the Russian

---

*Bergholz was the author of a diary of a visit to the court of St. Petersburg in the early part of the century. The diary, which was published in Büsching's Historical Magazine, contains nothing of special interest. His account of Catharine the First and her children has been reproduced on page 119.

language and religion gave way to instruction in the Swedish language and the Lutheran religion. But in November, 1741, Elizabeth Petrovna ascended the throne of the Romanoffs, and she very soon after wrote to her nephew desiring him to come to Russia and be brought up there as the heir to the throne. The young Prince received congratulations upon this auspicious event which proved in the end so terrible a misfortune.

Duke Peter came to St. Petersburg in 1742. The Empress received him with honor in the winter palace, celebrated his coming with festivities, and the people flocked to see their future Tzar. The following description has been given of him: "He was excessively pale and delicate looking; in short, everything in his appearance betokened the weakest constitution. The appearance of delicacy was enhanced by his blond hair, which hung down long in the fashion called Spanish. The evidences of feeble health were such as necessitated the immediate adoption of appropriate medical treatment."

The education which he had been receiving now underwent a slight change. He was instructed by Professor Stählin who became his head tutor, in history, mathematics, physics, moral philosophy and politics. He studied also Russian four times a week, and was with special diligence instructed in the dogmas of the Greek religion. When he had attained an adequate degree of proficiency in the latter, he was on the 17-18 November, 1742, received into the orthodox church, and an imperial manifesto proclaimed the Grand Duke Feodorovitch—as the Prince was now called—publicly and solemnly as the heir to the throne.

As soon as the Grand Duke was fifteen years old Elizabeth began to bethink her of finding him a wife. The choice of a bride for the now acknowledged heir to the Russian crown was an affair of moment. The various power-makers at the court of the Tzarina bestirred themselves to search for a bride who might prove advantageous to themselves, and the ambassadors of foreign courts began to consider the question of providing him with an Empress who should be favorable to their respective governments. The talk was now of an English, now of a French Princess. Elizabeth's choice fell first upon the Princess Sophia, of Zerbst, and next on the Princess Maria Anna, of Saxon-Poland, afterwards the wife of Maximiliam Joseph, Elector of Bavaria; then upon Amelia of Prussia, afterwards Abbess of Quedlinburg. The last two were unwilling to change their faith and declined the honor; but while the answer from the Saxon court was couched in very courteous language, the response from Berlin was scarcely civil. Frederick the Second wrote to Mandefeld, his Ambassador at St. Petersburg : " With regard to my sisters you know my views. I shall not marry any of them to Russia. I am surprised the Empress has not adhered to her choice of the Princess of Zerbst, she being of the Holstein family to which she is so much attached. In Hesse-Darmstadt also there are two princesses, one twenty and the other eighteen."

In March, 1743, Prince August von Holstein came to St. Petersburg, and it was not by accident that he brought with him a likeness of the Princess Sophia Augusta Frederika of Anhalt-Zerbst. The expressive face pleased the Empress; the Grand Duke also was well pleased with it. It was greatly in the young Princess's favor that she was the daughter of a Princess of Holstein, whose brother had been betrothed to Elizabeth but who died before the marriage took place. The project was favorably received, therefore, and early in December, 1743, Elizabeth sent Brümmer, the Grand Duke's Marshal, to invite the reigning Princess of Zerbst and her daughter to visit St. Petersburg and ten thousand rubles to defray the expenses of the journey.

In the beginning of February, 1744, the Princess and her daughter arrived in St. Petersburg, but the Court having two weeks before removed to Moscow, they remained there but a few days, after which they departed for the Kremlin city, arriving there on the evening of the 9th of February, the eve of the Grand Duke's birthday, which was the 10th. At the distance of three versts from the city they were met by Sievers, the lover and chamberlain of the Empress, bringing assurances that the Tzarina and Grand Duke were counting the minutes and hours until their arrival. They alighted at the wooden palace of Golovin where the Empress was residing. In the vestibule they were met by Brümmer and l'Estocq. They had no sooner entered their apartments, and before they had time to remove their furs and traveling cloaks, than the Grand Duke Peter entered and saluted the "dear guests in the most affectionate manner," as the Princess wrote in her letters home. A messenger immediately arrived from the Empress to the Grand Duke, desiring him to bring the princesses to the Empress's apartment, the sooner the better. In spite of the lateness of the hour the invitation was accepted. Elizabeth advanced to meet them, embraced and kissed them affectionately, and the Princess of Zerbst said : " I lay at the feet of Your Majesty my warmest gratitude, and venture to beg that you will continue your protection to the rest of my family, and to my daughter." The Tzarina answered : " What I have done is nothing compared with what I would like to do for your family, which is as dear to me as my own. My intentions will always remain the same, and you will judge best of my friendship by my actions."

They then proceeded to the sleeping chamber of the Empress, where an animated conversation continued until late in the night. The Tzarina gazed incessantly at the Princess, who bore a marked resemblance to her brother. The poor Tzarina was greatly affected and hurried into an adjoining chamber to indulge her feelings. When she was composed she returned to her guests.

Stählin, the Grand Duke's tutor, noted thus in his diary this memorable occasion .

"Arrival of the Princess of Anhalt-Zerbst and her daughter. The Empress enchanted."

Which was true. The Empress was at first

enchanted with the Princess of Zerbst, and loaded her and her daughter with costly presents.* Scarcely twenty-four hours after their arrival at Moscow, Elizabeth presented both ladies with the Order of Catharine, in the name of the Grand Duke, remarking that he had wished to ask for it of the Tzarina the day before, but had not ventured to do so.

The Princess of Zerbst was confounded by this mark of imperial favor and dazzled by the brilliancy and luxury with which the Empress had surrounded her and her daughter. " My daughter and I," she wrote to her husband, " live like queens; everything is laid with gold, and magnificent, our prospects are marvellous." They had their household, two chamberlains, two grooms of the chamber, four pages and a great number of servants.

The Princess Sophia made the most favorable impression upon the Empress, and the Princess of Zerbst could with truth write to her husband : " Notre fille trouve grande approbation. La souveraine la chérit, le successeur l'aime et c'est une affaire faite." And Catharine the

---

*Cipher dispatch of the Austrian Resident Count Hohenholz to Count Uhlfeld. Petersburg 29 Feb. 1744 new style. Vienna Court and State Archives. See Bilbassoff History of Katharine II. German Edition Berlin, 1891. Vol. Sec 2, Appendix I. Pages 35 and 40.

Second wrote subsequently in her Memoirs: "The Grand Duke seemed delighted at my arrival. At first he was very complaisant."

The impression which the Grand Duke made on the princess was also not unfavorable. A very friendly relation soon sprang up between them and an animated and confidential interchange of thoughts, plans, and wishes.

But it did not take long for the fifteen-year-old princess to discover that the sixteen-year-old prince was intellectually far behind her, that he was still in fact a mere child. But she had no wish to retreat. The future—the title of Empress of Russia—was too inviting. Soon, however, everything appeared to have lapsed into uncertainty, for the princess was taken very ill, and it was only by the utmost care that her life was rescued. Upon her recovery, the 29th of June, which was the anniversary of the Grand Duke's baptism, was fixed for the betrothal. On the day previous, the princess made the orthodox confession of faith. She appeared at the ceremonial in an adrienne robe of rose colored *gros de tours*, trimmed with silver lace, and with no ornament but a white band in her unpowdered hair, and by her very simplicity made the strongest impression upon all, men and women alike. In a clear, firm voice and in pure Russian, without a fault, she made her confession of faith. The St. Petersburg *News* said in its report of the great event, "It is impossible to describe the earnestness and grace with which this admirable Princess went through the solemn religious service; the most distinguished persons present, and the Empress herself, could not refrain from shedding tears of joy."

As a reward the devout young proselyte was presented by the Empress with a diamond agraffe, and a saint's picture in a case set with diamonds worth more than a hundred thousand rubles.

In the evening Catharine Alexejevna and the ladies of her court waited on the Grand Duke and presented him with a hunting equipment set with diamonds and emeralds.

After this they repaired to the Kremlin, where the next morning in the Cathedral of the Assumption a solemn betrothal was celebrated, following which Catharine received the title of Grand Duchess and Imperial Highness. The Empress herself placed the rings on the hands of the young pair, little marvels which cost together the sum of fifty thousand ducats. The event was closed by the firing of cannon and the ringing of bells, and an auspicious marriage appeared to have been inaugurated.

A few weeks after the betrothal, the Grand Duke fell suddenly ill with the smallpox, and it was not until some months later, in June 1745, that Catharine saw him again. "He had grown very much, and was almost unrecognizable," she says in her memoirs; "his features were very much enlarged, his whole face was marked and it was easy to see that the scars would remain. As his hair been cut off he wore a wig, which disfigured him still more. He came to me and asked me if I recognized him. I murmured some appropriate congratulations upon his recovery, but he had certainly grown frightfully ugly."

Catharine possessed so much self control and dissimulation that no one observed how repulsive her disfigured *fiance* had become to her. The Tzarina felt compassion for her, and exerted herself to divert the unfortunate bride elect. She surrounded her with cheerful companions with whom she might dance and be merry, and was very thoughtful and attentive. Peter, however, did nothing to attach Catharine to him, and concerned himself very little about her. He played soldiers with puppets, drilled rats, which he hanged if they were disobedient, and applied for instructions as to his prospective marriage to his groom of the chamber and favorite, Rumber. The latter informed him that a woman ought never to be permitted to contradict a man or to meddle with his affairs; if she opened her mouth to speak he should command her to be silent; he was the master in his house."

Catherine was deeply depressed. The conduct of her mother was a source of the keenest annoyance and vexation to her. The latter failed to comprehend her position at the court and mixed with political intrigues. Her immorality was worse still;* and as if to make good her own conduct she lent an ear to the insinuations of servants, with whom she was on terms of intimacy, and accused her daughter of visiting the Prince at night. Catharine thought of nothing less. She says: "This from my mother wounded me more than all. I told her it was an atrocious slander, at which she grew angry and drove me out of the room."

The presence of the Princess had long since grown irksome to the Empress and it is not to be wondered at that the English ambassador

---

* "Confidentially I have been informed that the old Princess of Zerbst is really pregnant." Cipher dispatch of Count Rosenburg to Count Uhlfield, dated Moscow, Nov. 16, 1774. Bilbassoff's History of Catharine II., Vol. I. Section 2. Appendix 1-6.

informed his court that the Empress was anxious to hasten the marriage in order to get rid of her with decency.

Preparations for the wedding were accordingly set on foot. It was to be celebrated with the utmost pomp. The Empress interested herself in the minutest details, and issued the following ukase: "We have endeavored that the Senate and all persons of rank should be notified of the marriage which is about to take place, in order that every one may be prepared with appropriate and as far as possible rich attire, as well as with the six-horse vehicles and other equipages. It is permitted to all on this solemn occasion to expend their precious things of gold and silver upon their apparel and equipages. And whereas this ceremony will be prolonged several days, and it is required of every person, man and woman, to be provided with at least one habit, they are permitted to cause to be prepared two or more of such habits; and also as every man is required to have in readiness one of the above mentioned equipages, he is permitted to have a second such equipage for his wife. The attendants upon such equipages will be according to rank, as follows: For persons of first and second class, two heyducs and eight lackeys; or, if any may desire, he may have twelve, but he may not have less than eight; two first-class runners, and, if any desire them, one or two pages in addition, and two chasseurs. For those of the third class every carriage must be accompanied by six lackeys and two runners; our chamberlains and chevaliers of the Court of the same rank, six servants: if any so desire they shall be entitled to have two runners. Persons of the fourth-rank class, and our chamberlains, as well as the chamberlains of their Imperial Highnesses shall have four servants. All others, both of the fifth and sixth-rank class, must be provided for this solemnity, if not during the ceremony, for the procession to our palace, with such apparel and equipage as beseems them."

There seems to have been a great scarcity of gold, and the German ambassador writes to his court: "Money and credit are so scarce that it is difficult to obtain loans to procure even the stuff for the liveries and laces, not to speak of other more expensive matters."

Nevertheless all sped well. All the foreign courts prescribed regulations for the ceremony, and from Dresden and Paris came piles of descriptions of marriages, sometimes accompanied by illustrations.

In the middle of August heralds in armor

accompanied by soldiers of the guard and dragoons rode through the streets of St. Petersburg with drums, and announced to the people that the marriage would take place on the 21st of August in the Kasan Church. Fountains of wine and festal boards were set up in front of the palace, and splendid preparations for the visitor were made in all the streets. In the harbor were seen gayly decked galleys and yachts, prepared to accompany the ceremony with the firing of guns.

At seven in the morning the bride waited upon the Empress to be dressed for the marriage. Elizabeth placed on her unpowdered hair a small crown of diamonds. The bride's gown was silver-glacé bordered with gold. She looked enchanting, more beautiful perhaps than ever she looked before or after. At ten the bridal procession left the palace for the church. Cuirassiers, guards, dragoons and hussars accompanied the 120 magnificent equipages. The Empress rode with the bridal pair in a carriage drawn by eight horses. "The procession," said the English ambassador, "was the most magnificent that was ever known in this country, and infinitely surpassed anything I ever saw."

The crowd of people on foot was so great that

the Empress and the bridal pair did not reach the church until one o'clock. There, with extraordinary pomp the ceremony took place. In the course of his remarks the confessor of the ducal pair said: "I perceive the finger of Providence in the union of these two."

Masquerades, balls and fireworks followed, and "amid the most joyous festival that ever took place in Europe," as the Princess of Zerbst wrote to her husband, the most unhappy of royal marriages was solemnized.

Catharine speaks of it thus:

"My dear husband concerned himself very little about me. For my part I yawned and was bored." *

After his marriage the heir to the throne continued the same as before; nor did he change later. In his 28th year he still played with puppets. His passion for playing with puppets was only second to his passion for drink.

Of love or of marital relations there was no question. Nearly a year passed and Elizabeth saw no prospect of the fulfilment of her hope of an heir to the throne. At last she felt herself

---

* Mon cher epoux ne s'occupait nullement de moi, mais était continuellement avec ses valets, a jouer aux militaires, les exercant dans sa chambre ou changeant l'uniforme vingt fois par jour. Je baillais, je m'ennuyais." * * * Mémoires. 47.

constrained to provide the Grand Duchess with an extra lady in waiting for the purpose of "promoting conjugal intimacy between their Imperial Highnesses." *

A cousin of the Empress, Madam Marja Ssimonovna Tschogolof, was chosen for this delicate post. She was young, scarcely twenty-four, very pretty, and at that time virtuous. She loved her husband and had a number of children. She was therefore fitted to teach by example.

---

*The instructions given to this lady were as follows: "Whereas Her Imperial Highness the Grand Duchess has been chosen to be the worthy spouse of our dear nephew, His Imperial Highness the Grand Duke and Heir of this Empire, and has been elevated to her present dignity of Imperial Highness, with the intent and hope that Her Imperial Highness, by her discretion and virtues would incline his heart to a sincere love and would thereby bestow upon the Empire the wished-for heir and successor to our most High Imperial house; as this, however, cannot be attained without the groundwork of mutual affection and conjugal intimacy, especially without a complete conformity to the character of the Prince, we cherish the gracious hope that Her Imperial Highness, bearing in mind that her own happiness and welfare depend thereon, will not fail carefully to consider this important object and for the accomplishment of it will on her side use the utmost complaisance and every possible means. Yourself we most strictly command to be zealous in using every occasion to remind Her Imperial Highness and earnestly to urge upon her and engage her to consort with her husband in a manner the most

Catharine, however, was not to blame for the existing relations.* She said in speaking of the Grand Duke: "S'il avait voulu etre aimé la chose n'aurait pas été difficile pour moi."

That Catharine was naturally inclined to her conjugal duties and fitted for the performance of them was afterwards sufficiently proved.

The kind of husband that Peter was is illustrated by the following circumstance which occurred in the fifth year of his married life. He fancied a Princess of Courland, with regard

---

friendly and affectionate, to encourage him by complaisance, consideration, love, friendship and ardent devotion, and in general to do everything to prevent a certain coldness, to avoid wounding him, and thereby to procure for herself and her husband the sweetest life and to us the wished-for fulfilment of this, our useful motherly purpose, and to realize the heartfelt wish of all our true subjects. To this end you are to use the utmost care to promote to the greatest possible degree intimate acquaintance and good understanding and the most sincere and lasting affection and marital confidence." * * * See Bilbassoff, History of Catharine the Second, Vol. I, 265.

*In regard to her childlessness Catharine expressed herself with sadness in a letter of the 24th of April 1774 to Madam von Bjelke (Magazine of the Russian Historical Society VII, 100). See Catharine's Memoirs 117,162. Castera speaks of an "imperfection" of Peter's (see Life of Catharine I, 49). Brückner who weighs everything so carefully, is of the opinion that Castera's statement coincides with the facts·

to whom Catharine concealed as best she could her indignation and wounded vanity. One night when she had retired and had just fallen asleep the Grand Duke entered, in a state of hilarious intoxication. He began dilating on the charms and beauty of the Princess of Courland, and as Catharine did not respond and was about to fall asleep again, he boxed her ears and then retired, content and happy.

In spite of his infirmity he did not wish to be behind his courtiers in the matter of intrigues.* His first "love" was the Princess of Courland. This inclination was short-lived; she gave place to a Miss Schapiroff who again made way for a Miss Teploff. Lastly Elizabeth Romanovna Woronzoff appeared, whom Catharine speaks of in her memoirs as the favorite Sultana. As Peter showed himself foolish in

---

*The question whether Catharine not only tolerated but promoted Peter's love affairs has been much contested. See de la Marche: Nouveaux mémoires ou anecdotes du règne et du détronement de Pierre III. Berlin et Dresde 1765. 225. The brother of Elizabeth Romanovna Woronzoff has remarked in his autobiography that Catharine tried to control Peter's choice of his mistresses and to rule them; when Schapiroff became too independent, Catharine replaced her by Woronzoff, and when Woronzoff acquired too much power she sought to remove her. Archiv des Fürsten Woronzoff, 20-21. Brückner 42-43.

everything, so he chose as the partners of his amours the ugliest women of the court. Elizabeth superabounded in ugliness. She was pockmarked, thick-set and dumpy, and without intelligence or animation. Nevertheless she exercised the greatest influence over Peter.

It is easy to understand that Catharine did not feel drawn toward such a husband as this. In a letter to a friend she thus expresses herself with regard to the unhapy Queen Caroline Matilda of Denmark. "Nothing can be worse than to have a child for a husband. I know it, and it is my opinion that when women do not love their husbands it is the fault of the latter. I would have loved mine if it had been possible, and if he had the goodness to desire it." In a journal of the year 1761 we find the folfowing: "A man who shows enmity toward us and withholds from us our due, severs the bond between us and cancels the obligation which this bond lays upon us," an expression aimed directly at her husband and which shows how deeply her feelings were aroused against him.

It was deplorable, and it was nothing bettered when they ascended the throne. The gulf between them went on widening. In a manifesto published by Peter the day he became Emperor, not the most distant mention was made of Catharine. Not much of a trustworthy nature is known as to the personal relations of the imperial pair. The Empress came every morning to the Emperor's cabinet but remained only a moment. At dinner she did not appear at the table; in her place came the Countess Woronzoff who had been made lady of the bedchamber, not however to the Tzarina; her apartments joined those of the Tzar.

Breteuil, the French Ambassador, wrote to his government in January, 1762: "When we went to offer our congratulations we found the Tzarina looking very much dejected. It is evident that she will exercise no influence, and she is, I think, trying to arm herself with philosophy. But her character is not adapted to it although she often assures me of the contrary. The Emperor has redoubled his attentions to Woronzoff. She resides at the Court and is treated with the greatest distinction. A most remarkable choice, it must be confessed." At another time he wrote: "The position of the Empress is cruel. She is treated with the most conspicuous contempt. She endures the conduct of the Emperor and the arrogance of Miss Woronzoff with great patience. I cannot but believe that the Empress, whose courage and violence of character I know, will sooner or later be driven to some act of desperation. She has friends who if she wished it would dare everything for her. * * * The Empress is winning universal favor. No one shows more zeal in paying the last duties to the deceased Empress. She observes with the most scrupulous exactness all the anniversaries and fasts, the rules for fasting, and everything of that nature, which the Emperor treats lightly, although they are not matters of indifference to the Russian people. In a word, she neglects nothing that tends to please, and pays too much attention to everything that is conducive to that end for self-love not to have a share in it. She is not a woman to forget the threat that was so often in Peter's mouth when he was Grand Duke, that when he became Emperor he would shut her up as Peter the First had shut up his wife. All this, joined to daily humiliations, must be fermenting in a brain like hers and only waiting the opportunity to burst forth. * * * The health of the Empress is so broken by grief and anxiety that the worst is to be feared."

The antagonism between Catharine and Peter became more and more evident. Breteuil wrote : " The Empress has courage both of soul and mind and is as much respected as the Emperor is hated and despised." And again : " The Empress is subjected to personal insults from her husband, which she answers only with respect and tears. The people suffer with her and do not spare their unavailing good wishes."

The English Ambassador, Keith, who was in general more favorably disposed to Peter than his contemporaries, writes of the position of Catharine at this time : " It does not seem that the Empress has thus far often been asked for her opinion, or that she enjoys much consideration." * * * She did not appear at the court balls, and Mercy reported that "she does not wish to witness the disorderly and indecent conduct that prevails, and remains shut up in her room where she spends her time bitterly weeping."

This may have been true, but that the cause assigned was the correct one, may be doubted. Catharine had long since ceased to be a prude. It was not long after this that her son, by Orloff, the future Count Bobrinsky, was born.

The memoirs of the jeweler, Pauzié, throw a sharp flash of light on the married life of the imperial pair. Pauzié says the Emperor forbade him to deliver anything to the Empress, although at this time Catharine did not make heavy demands for ornaments, she often wanted for necessaries, and was entirely without pocket money. Peter carried his petty hatred so far as to forbid the gardener to supply her with a particular fruit which she liked. Naturally the court ladies no longer showed her the respect due to their sovereign.

Count Hordt, in his "Memoirs of a Swedish Gentleman," tells how upon one occasion while he was conversing with Catharine the Emperor drew him abruptly away and led him to a table where he was carousing with Miss Woronzoff. Hordt remarked that Catharine exhibited on the occasion much tact, but could with difficulty conceal her "deep dejection."

At a grand dinner given by Peter in honor of the peace concluded with Prussia, he sent his adjutant to ask Catharine why she did not respond to the toast he had proposed. "I did not think it necessary," answered Catharine. The answer enraged him and he struck her in the face across the table. Every one was stupefied and Catharine burst into tears; but recovering herself quickly she conversed with her neighbor in an animated manner as if nothing had occurred.

Such were the relations of the imperial pair, while the influence of Miss Woronzoff increased daily. Her credit was such that even at foreign courts, and especially at the Court of Berlin, great efforts were made to secure her favor. Goltze wrote to his sovereign : " It would be greatly to the advantage of Your Majesty if you would present Miss Woronzoff with a bouquet of diamonds in the form of an espalier." That was too costly a tune for Frederick the Second. He answered the Ambassador wittily in his own handwriting : " Where, diable, would you have me get bouquets of diamonds the size of espaliers? Do you not know that my country is ruined?"

Great as appears to have been the influence of Miss Woronzoff, it was far from being as great as that of the favorites of the former Tzarinas, or of Catharine the Second, and it was not injurious to the Empire. A woman cannot under the government of a man, even the most despicable of men, obtain such power as a man may under the government of a woman. Elizabeth Romanovna received from the Tzar only insignificant presents. While the favorites of Elizabeth and Catharine the Second filched hundreds of millions from the people, Elizabeth Romanovna obtained only an insignificant landed estate, a few diamonds, and a house of which Catharine deprived her after the murder of Peter.

So infatuated was Peter with Miss Woronzoff that he wished on her account to repudiate his wife. Everything was at stake for Catharine. It was necessary to act promptly.

Peter became more and more odious, his mistress grew every day more insolent and the Emperor abandoned himself to the most scandalous excesses with her and with other "ladies," smoking and drinking with them until they dropped under the table. By the side of princesses were to be seen wenches and dancing girls who were invited to take part in these orgies, and when the former remonstrated, Peter answered: "there are no distinctions of rank among women."

The Russians had endured with patience Elizabeth's debaucheries because they respected in her the blood of Peter the Great, but with Peter the Third, a foreigner, a Holsteiner, they began to show themselves restive. They were anxious to be rid of the Emperor and Catharine found her task easy.

She was more crafty than he. While he, the Emperor of Russia, wounded his people by his exaggerated love for Germany, she, the German-born princess showed herself always the most uncompromising of Russians. She was careful to observe all the orthodox ceremonies, and never absented herself from church. If she met a beggar she had for him words of solace; the soldiers she addressed in friendly terms and offered her hand to the lowliest to kiss. Withal she exhibited the most touching patience. She was seldom heard to complain, and thereby excited still more the popular interest and compassion. Only at times at a public festival, the long pent up tears would seem involuntarily to overflow her beautiful eyes. The comedies thus played by her were better than those she wrote, and won a more signal success.

Catharine found her accomplice in the Princess Dashkoff, one of the most interesting figures of her epoch. She was the beautiful* sister of the ugly Elizabeth Romanovna Woron-

---

* She is reputed to have been very beautiful, although Diderot, who, however, it must be said, saw her in her latter years, has not drawn a brilliant picture of her personal appearance. He says: "The Princess is not in least beautiful. She is small, has an open brow, round puffed-out cheeks, eyes neither small nor large and rather deep set, dark hair and brows, a rather flat nose, a large mouth, thick lips, a long round neck of the national type, a broad chest and not much of a figure. Her movements are without grace." He further says that the Princess

zoff, and like her was reared at her uncle's house. The following account of her marriage will illustrate the energy of her character.

Prince Dashkoff was paying his court to her at a ball in a rather lively fashion, when she suddenly called to her uncle, the Grand Chancellor:

"My dear uncle, Prince Dashkoff has just done me the honor to ask for my hand."

Dashkoff was struck dumb with amazement, informed him that the revolution of 1762 was almost accomplished before Catharine had any suspicion of it!

The Princess was a revolutionary enthusiast, in that day a phenomenon. At the age of nineteen she entered the field of politics like a veteran diplomat. To her more than to all the rest who took part in it combined, is to be attributed the successful issue of Catharine's revolution.

Madam Dashkoff became subsequently the Director of the Academy of Sciences, and amusing anecdotes are told of her parsimony in this position. In the winter she would not permit the salons to be heated, although she exacted the regular attendance of members at the meetings. Many renounced their membership sooner than be forced to listen for hours to scientific discussions in an ice-house. She attended them herself wrapped in a number of fur robes. She appeared to regard savans in the light of soldiers, and to have the disposition, like Peter the Great, to enforce education with the whip. She left memoirs which were first published in 1757 in London by Alexander Herzen, and subsequently in Hamburg by Hoffman & Campe. In spite of their vain garrulousness they are well worthy of perusal.

but he did not dare to say to the Grand Chancellor and favorite of the Tzarina that he was merely paying his compliments to the lady and was not thinking of marriage. Immediately the young lady received congratulations on all sides, and before the Prince knew it he was married. After the event, however, he showed himself the master and sent his wife to reside at Moscow.*

Very soon after Elizabeth Romanovna Woronzoff became the mistress of Peter, the Princess returned hastily from Moscow to reap the benefits of her sister's liaison.

Catharine, aware of the ambition of the Princess Dashkoff and that she was panting to play an equally important rôle with that of her ugly and nevertheless influential sister, had little difficulty in winning the young Princess to her cause. Sister against sister, Empress against Emperor, these were the foremost characters in the play of intrigue which met with a swift success and ended in the downfall of Peter and his mistress.

One day the Emperor, accompanied by his "chubby Woronzoff," as the Russian Pompadour was styled, while on the way from his

---

*The Princess informs us that she made a love marriage and that the Prince was infatuated with her.

pleasure palace Oranienbaum to a ball at Peterhof, learned that his wife, who had been residing there, had suddenly disappeared. While the Emperor was rioting with his mistress Catharine had gone quietly to the capital and set the revolt regularly upon the stage. Before Peter could take in clearly what was happening, and while he and Woronzoff were expressing to each other their astonishment, a messenger arrived, dispatched by a faithful servant with the news that the guards had revolted and that Catharine had been proclaimed the reigning sovereign.

Instead of making a bold and final attempt to save himself, the Tzar crept timidly under his mistress's skirts, and on receiving a summons from Catharine to abdicate, he instantly complied, requesting only that he and Woronzoff might be permitted to leave the country unmolested.

The few who had thus far remained faithful to him soon deserted this ridiculous figure, and instead of being permitted to quit the country he was brought to Ropscha, the estate of Gregor Orloff. For company, he was given by his own request his physician Luders, his violin, his negro Narcissus, and his favorite dog. He was murdered at Ropscha on the 5-16 of July, in which event Alexis Orloff bore the principal part.

The chubby Woronzoff relapsed into the obscurity out of which the Emperor's caprice had raised her to the steps of a throne. She was taken to Moscow and married later the Brigadier Poljansky.

It has often been assumed that Peter was murdered by Catharine's order, as evidence of which it is alleged that she showed no consternation upon being informed of it. For that, however, there was no cause. There is no reason to question the accuracy of the account of this occurrence which Princess Dashkoff has given in her memoirs. She says:

"If any one is malicious enough to impute to the Empress a participation in the murder of her husband, or even a knowledge of it, absolute proof of the injustice of such a suspicion is to be found in a letter still extant from Alexis Orloff to the Empress, written by his own hand a few minutes after the horrible act was accomplished. The style and disconnectedness of it, even when allowance is made for his state of intoxication, show the horror and frenzy of his mental condition as he implores her pardon for his act. This important letter was preserved by Catharine with great care in a casket of valuable papers which Prince Desborodko after the death of the Empress examined by

Paul's orders and read aloud. When he had concluded the reading Paul made the sign of the cross and exclaimed:' God be praised! every doubt which I entertained as to the conduct of my mother in this regard, is dispelled.' The Empress and Miss Nelidoff were present on the occasion, and the Emperor ordered that the letter should also be read in the presence of the Grand Duke and of Count Rostopschin. To those who honor the name of Catharine nothing will be more grateful than this discovery, and although I did not need the evidence for my own conviction, still no other circumstance of my life has given me greater satisfaction than the certainty that a document such as this exists, capable of silencing forever the foul slander which would stain the reputation of a sovereign who with all her weaknesses was incapable even of entertaining the thought of such a crime."

Peter died uncrowned. Thirty-five years after his death Paul caused his coffin to be opened and the body to be solemnly crowned.*

---

*Memoirs of the Life and Reign of Peter the Third. Dorpat 1762. Lebensgeschichte Peters des Dritten 1762. Frankfurt and Leipzig. Jean Goebel, Fragmens historiques sur Pierre III. et Catharina II. History and anecdotes of Peter III, by de la Marche, London, 1776. Comte de Hordt, Lettres sur la Russie par un Gentilhomme Suédois. Merkwürdige Lebensgeschischte des unglücklichen Russischen Kaisers Peter III. Anekdoten zur Lebensgeschichte des Fürsten Orlow. Interressante Lebensgemählde, von Samuel Baur, V. Coxe, Reise durch Polen, Russland. Zurich, 1785. Histoire de Pierre III, imprimée sur un manuscrit trouvé dans les papiers de Montmorin ancien ministre des affaires étrangères et composé par un agent secret de Louis XV. a la cour de Petersbourg. Suivie de l'histoire des amours et principaux amans de Catharine II. Paris an VII. Saldern, Biography of Peter the Third from an unpartisan examination of the Revolution of that period. Petersburg, 1800. Biographie Peters des Dritten (von Helbig), Tübingen, Cotta, 1808. Russische Anecdoten oder Briefe eines teutschen Offiziers an einen Livländischen Edelmann. Wansbeck, 1765. Rulhière, Anecdotes sur la révolution de Russie en 1762. Paris, 1807. Feyerliche Dankrede des Erzbischofs von Gross-Nowgorod auf die Entthronung Peters III. Wien, 1762. Briefe Peters III, an Friedrich den Grossen. Russkaja Starina, 1871-3. Oeuvres posthumes de Frédéric IV tome. Du péril de la balance politique de l'Europe. Mémoires pour servir a l'histoire de Pierre III, par Mr. D. H. Extraits de l'histoire de Pierre III, Avec plusieurs anecdotes singulières. Urkunden and Materialien zur Kenntnis der nordischen Reiche, 1786. Allerneueste geheime Nachrichten vom Russische Hofe, 1766. Bülau, geheime Geschichten und räthselhafte Menschen Leipzig, 1863, Bd. I, 1-58. See in addition the works quoted upon Elizabeth and Catharine the Second.

CATHARINE THE SECOND AND HER FAVORITES.

Catharine's marriage.—Her first intrigue with Ssaltykoff, her husband's chamberlain.—The birth of Prince Paul.—Ssaltykoff's fall.—Poniatowski becomes Catharine's favorite.—The discovery of this relation.—Poniatowski's banishment.—Gregor Orloff.—His great power.—Project of marriage to the Tzarina.—His fall.—His and Catharine's children.—Alexis Orloff, the murderer of Peter the Third.—A recruit, an officer and a nobleman, favorites of the Tzarina.—The functions of a favorite.—His duties and his pay.—Potemkin becomes favorite.—His tyranny over the Tzarina.—His end as favorite.—Potemkin becomes minister.—His death.—Other favorites: Savadovsky, Soritsch, Korsakoff, Lanskoi, Jermaloff, Mamonoff and Suboff.—Catharine's end.

CATHARINE THE SECOND was not only the most famous, but also the most dissolute princess of her time. An account of all of her liaisons would be irksome; I will confine myself to the most prominent.

The court, the nobles, the burghers and the lowest classes, all were in a state of the most complete moral dilapidation. Love adventures, if the term may be applied to the most revolting libertinism, played the principal rôle at this Court, and at the head of this debased society was the Empress herself. The young Grand Duchess had not only before her eyes accidental and unpremeditated examples of licentious manners—her attendants, and the companions chosen for her, were women of the worst reputation. The Grand Duke was himself constantly occupied with his amours, for notwithstanding his physical unfitness to be a husband, he was sensually attracted toward such women as he made the companions of his debauches. It often happened that Catharine and the Grand Duke's mistresses encountered each other, and scandalous scenes would ensue, the mistresses acting in an insolent manner toward the wife. In such a Court and under such conditions Catharine would scarcely have remained pure and innocent had she been as modest and good as an angel, and this she was not. She early learned the art of dissimulation, and became more proficient in the practice of it than any one else at the Court. She had also more need of it. In her relations with her mother, the Empress, and her husband, the utmost caution and dissembling were necessary. Every step must be calculated, every action cunningly weighed, all open-heartedness suppressed. The Grand Duke busied himself with hanging rats and playing with puppets. Catharine was vigorous and had need of physical activity. She took refuge in riding and dancing, which only strengthened her and aroused still more her sensual nature.

We need not wonder that she fell, but rather that she remained virtuous so long.

The marital relations of the Grand Duke and Grand Duchess were no secret at the Court, and in such circumstances many dared to lift their eyes to the unhappy Grand Duchess. Although at first they were repulsed, there were many who suspected her of secret relatious with this person or that. Those accustomed to that atmosphere of the lowest immorality could not believe that the wife of such a husband lived without intrigues. Catharine had been so long suspected that she began to believe in her own guilt, and launched out finally in the career of vice.

It is characteristic that when Elizabeth was informed of Catharine's first confidant, a chamber lackey, Tschernyschoff, she promoted him to be an officer and sent him to Orenberg. The day that Tschernyschoff was removed, the Empress charged Madam Tschoglokoff with the task of promoting conjugal intimacy between the Grand Ducal pair.

Madam Tschoglokoff was not however equal to the occasion. She not only did not promote conjugal intimacy, she did not even remark that under her very eyes the courtiers were one after the other falling in love with Catharine, and that one after the other was successful in winning her favor, her own husband being amongst those who prostrated themselves at Catharine's feet.

In 1749 the court of the Grand Duke was at the poor little palace of Rajevo. Here Count Kirill Rasumovsky, a brother of Elizabeth's favorite and husband, often came to visit. When Catharine asked him what brought him so frequently to their wretched nest, he answered : "Love."

"But with whom can you be in love here?"

"With whom ? With you."

Catharine says in her memoirs twenty years after in recalling this episode : "I laughed heartily, for I had never in the least suspected that he could be in love with me."

She soon heard more of it.

On one occasion Tschoglokoff, the husband of her overseer, fell at her feet and poured out his ardent passion ; but he was "too stout, too stupid and too impudent, with a mind as heavy as his body, and I silenced him." Sachar Grigorjevitch Tschernyscheff met with better success. He was young, witty, animated and neither stout nor impudent, and he pleased Catharine. He understood the art of soft flattery, he sent her tender verses, and he did not find her insensible. Once she tells us, "he begged me to grant him an interview in my chamber or some other place. I answered that it was quite impossible, my chamber was inaccessible and I could not leave it. He said he would disguise himself as a servant, but I positively refused." And she assures us that this ended the matter. This seems improbable in view of the passionate letters which have been discovered adressed by her to Count Sachar Grigorjevitch. At all events a predisposition to gallantry was awakened and the next one was not refused.

This was Ssergey Ssaltykoff, the friend and chamberlain of the Grand Duke.

Although quite young, Ssaltykoff had already numerous adventures behind him. He was a hero as regards the conquest of women ; in such warfare he shrank neither from the heat of battle nor from patient endurance, and did not hesitate to enter the lists either with the most virtuous of wives or the discreetest of maidens. If, however, in the neighborhood of the lady he was storming a protector or an avenger rose up, he quickly vanished and sought precipitately a place of safety.

Ssaltykoff had married for love a pretty lady in waiting to the Empress, named Matrjona Pawlovna Balk. But he no sooner found himself in the place of chamberlain to the Grand Duke than he fell in love with Catharine, upon observing how unhappy in her marriage was the pretty Grand Duchess. He remarked how she was dying of ennui at Oranienbaum, which place Elizabeth had assigned to the young couple for a residence, he knew that nature had not fitted her for a life of quite contemplation but had inclined her to activity, pleasure and excitement, and believed himself capable of enlivening and contenting her. He induced the Grand Duke to give balls, busied himself in arranging entertaining programmes, and was careful when the Grand Duchess expressed her pleasure and surprise, to designate himself as the author of these amusements, designed expressly for her.

This pleased the Grand Duchess.

At a concert at the residence of the overseer, Madam Tschoglokoff, Saltykoff poured out his ardent passion. But the affair dragged, and wishing to bring matters to a crisis Saltykoff feigned the necessity to depart on a journey and showed the strongest emotion, even wept, in prospect of the separation. Catharine was affected by the comedy, asked why he must go, begged him not to remain long absent, confessed her love, and the "bond of noble souls" was formed.

Wishing to be left undisturbed with her lover, when the Grand Duke was about to make a journey to St. Petersburg she feigned illness and Peter went alone, leaving behind him his friend and chamberlain Saltykoff. For Catharine's illness he was the best physician.

Ssaltykoff gradually forgot to be prudent, and the affair began to attract attention. The virtuous Empress Elizabeth discovered the relation and became very indignant, but Catharine succeeded in assuaging her wrath. The watch kept by Madame Tschoglokoff had profited nothing. Meanwhile the latter herself caught the contagion and fell in love with Prince Ivan Petrovitch Repnin. Happily for the enamoured Madam Tscholokoff, her husband soon after died and left the lovers a clear field.

Alexander Ivanovitch Schuvaloff, a near relative of Elizabeth's favorite, was chosen to fill the place of the Grand Duke's late seneschal. It was not a very happy choice for Catharine, who was then pregnant by Ssaltykoff. Not only on his own account, but by reason of the position which he held as the head of the imperial inquisitorial court, called the "secret chancery," Alexander Schuvaloff was the terror of the court, the city and the whole empire. In addition to this his personal appearance was repulsive, and he had a nervous twitching of his face which caused him to make the most horrible grimaces.

Toward the end of August, 1754, Catharine was approaching her confinement. Little attention appears to have been paid to her. She was then residing with her husband at the summer palace at St. Petersburg where she had two rooms in a remote part of the palace; two long bare and scantily furnished rooms, and here, on the 20th of September, Paul Ssergewitch—I ask pardon—Petrovitch, was born. The child, the wished for heir, was immediately taken from the young mother and the latter was left quite alone and neglected in the sick chamber, while the Grand Duke drank with his lackeys and mistresses. While the Empress occupied herself with the infant Catharine groaned and wept, but no one paid any heed to her.

After the baptism of the Prince the Empress came one day at last into the apartments of the Grand Duchess, bringing her on a gold platter a present of a hundred thousand rubles and a necklace, rings and earrings. Catharine was delighted with the money, for she had many debts, but of the ornaments she remarks in her memoirs: "I would have been ashamed to have made such a present to my chambermaid."

Moreover, her delight in the money was short-lived. Four days after, the secretary of the Empress came to her, saying: "In heaven's name lend me the money for the Empress." Catharine reluctantly consented and never saw it again.

Immediately after Paul's birth his real father Ssergey Ssaltykoff was sent to Sweden.*

---

*Catherine asserts in her memoirs that Elizabeth was accessory to her relations with Ssaltykoff in order to provide a "lawful" heir to the throne. The heir had appeared, and Ssaltykoff must disappear. Mémoires 169, 170. See Blum, J. J. Sievers IV. 267. Jauffret I. 79. Brückner, 42, thinks that Catharine in making this assertion was playing a trump card against Paul to deprive him of the succession.

The banishment of her lover caused Catharine the greatest distress. She was in despair, and for weeks did not quit her chamber. It was not until the fortieth day after the birth of the Prince that she made her appearance. She says: "Je le trouvai fort beau et sa vue me réjouit un peu." But she saw him for a moment only, for he was taken away from her by Elizabeth.

This solicitude of Elizabeth for the child and her disregard of the mother put the latter out of humor, and gave rise to reports that Catharine's child had been exchanged for a child of Elizabeth's. Catharine again found herself alone as before, with neither the love of husband or child to occupy her and driven more and more to illicit love. Ssaltykoff, it is true, returned from Sweden, but was immediately sent to Hamburg and not permitted to remain in St. Petersburg.

At first Catharine was inconsolable, but learning that Ssaltykoff had found solace in other women she followed his example.* He

---

* "Environ ce temps-la j'appris comme quoi la conduite de Serge Saltikoff avait été peu mesurée. Outre cela il en avait conté a toutes les femmes qu'il avait rencontrées. Au commencement je ne voulais rien en croire mais a la fin je l'entendis répéter de tant de côtés, que ses amis memes ne purent le disculper." Mémoires da l'impératrice Catherine IIe. Londres 1859, 240.

had proved himself unworthy of her love, and she began to look about for some more worthy object.

She did not look long.

In the beginning of July, 1775, the English ambassador, Sir Charles Hanbury Williams, arrived at St. Petersburg and presented himself at the Grand Duke's Court at Oranienbaum. In his suite was Count Poniatowski, a Pole, young, amiable, clever and good looking. "In appearance only Ssaltykoff could be compared with him," said Catharine, "and in mind he was his superior." The Count had no sooner seen the Grand Duchess than he fell in love with her, and he understood so well the art of being tender and captivating that he found Catharine an easy prey.

It was one of Catharine's characteristics that she did not desire her lovers to risk anything in obtaining access to her. Disguising herself therefore as a man she went herself boldly on winter nights to the English Embassy. After this had been often repeated, it became necessary to contrive a new and less dangerous tryst. The opportunity was furnished by Peter himself.

The Grand Duke, who had apparently as little suspicion of the new liaison of his wife as he had of the old one, was so completely captivated by Poniatowski's artfully feigned admiration for Frederick the Great, that he found his society indispensable, and when the Polish government suddenly recalled the Count to Warsaw, the Grand Duke bestirred himself to cause him to be sent back to St. Petersburg. He was successful. Poniatowski obtained the position of Polish Ambassador to the Russian court, and Peter had now once more his congenial companion, and Catharine her lover.

In the night of the 8–9 of December, 1757, Catharine became aware that she was about to be delivered of a child. The Grand Duke, Count Schuvaloff, and the Empress were notified. In a short while the Grand Duke presented himself in the uniform of a Holstein officer, with boots, spurs, scarf and sword. Catharine, astonished, asked what all that parade meant at such an hour. Peter the Foolish answered:

"Real friends can be known only in important moments. In this uniform I will fulfil my duty as a Holstein officer and protect the house of Holstein, according to my oath. You are ill, Imperial Highness; I have hastened to render you assistance." He was drunk. Twenty-four hours later a girl was born, who was called Anna, and incorrectly styled Anna Petrovna.

The Grand Duke knew already that Catharine was not his wife alone. Catharine assures us that he once said in presence of the court: "Dieu sait ou ma femme prend ses grossesses; je ne sait pas trop si cet enfant est a moi et s'il faut que je le prenne sur mon compte."

Nevertheless, he feigned great satisfaction at the child's birth, and sent express messengers to his relatives to inform them of the "joyful" event.

Not long after, his suspicions being aroused and having become watchful of the Pole's good fortune, he surprised him in the company of the Grand Duchess disguised as a hair dresser. But his wrath was short-lived. Catharine represented to him that a public scandal would be incompatible with his dignity, and reminded him that he was not himself a pattern of conjugal fidelity but maintained open relations with Woronzoff, and Peter the Foolish was base enough to acquiesce and allow Catharine and her gallant to go free, and, so far as he was concerned, matters went on as before.

Not so mild in her judgments, however, was the virtuous Elizabeth. She insisted upon banishing Poniatowski from the Court. He returned to Warsaw, and led for some time an obscure existence. But when Catharine, with whom he was in constant correspondence, became sovereign, his good fortune returned and the period of his fame began.

Although Catharine had since Poniatowski's banishment given her heart away several times, she had so much feeling still left for the handsome Pole that it was for a time believed she would marry him. It did not come to that, however, but to console him for not giving him her hand she rewarded her lover with the sovereignty of his native country. Neither before him nor after him has any princess bestowed so dazzling a reward for so obscure a service.

The parvenu showed himself altogether unworthy of a throne, and no one can feel much compassion for the contemptible destiny procured for him by the same Empress who had raised him so high.

Poniatowski was indebted for his successful career to nothing but his beauty. He passed for one of the handsomest men of his day. He had a stately figure, an affable and insinuating address, and much goodness of heart. His character was weak, almost timid; he was unequal to any high undertaking, fitted only for the petty life of a court and the society of voluptuous women. He was, therefore, a favorite of fortune so long as he moved in the sphere to which he was adapted, but he met with swift shipwreck when he attempted to guide a great ship of state. *

The immediate successor of Poniatowski in Catharine's favor was Gregor Orloff. An Orloff had already distinguished himself in the reign of Peter the Great. The following anecdote is related of him:

When Peter was punishing the revolt of the Streltzi it happened that a young man belonging to this daring militia, named Ivan Orell (John the Eagle), when his turn came to lay his head on the block put aside with his foot the head of a comrade which was in his way, remarking: "I must make room for myself here." Peter, who was usually present at

---

* On November 15, 1795, Stanilaus Augustus was compelled to abdicate the throne, which he had in fact only filled for Catharine. The Russian Government undertook the payment of his debts of three millions of ducats, and gave him a pension of two hundred thousand ducats, of which Prussia and Austria contributed forty thousand. Until the death of Catharine he remained in Grodno. Paul I summoned him to St. Petersburg, where he passed his last days peacefully enough in the circle of the Imperial family and in the society of his compeers. He died on the 12th of February, 1798.

executions, was so much astonished at this humor of the gallows that he pardoned the young man and placed him as a common soldier in a regiment of the line. Ivan rose by his courage to the rank of officer and noble.

His son in his thirty-fifth year married a girl of sixteen, and in spite of this advanced age became the father of nine sons, the second and third of whom were Gregor and Alexis Orloff. Both were uncommonly handsome, an advantage which at the St. Petersburg court opened up to them a brilliant career.

Count Peter Schuvaloff the master of ordnance, who was vain and ostentatious, wished to have as his adjutant the handsomest officer that could be found. Gregor Orloff then serving in an artillery regiment was presented to him. He pleased the general and was given the position. Schuvaloff had now not only the handsomest officer for his adjutant but the most beautiful woman in the capital, the Princess Jelena Stepanovna, for his mistress. The most beautiful woman fell in love with the handsomest man, and the mistress and adjutant amused themselves behind the General's back until the betrayed lover surprised them and brought the tender idyl to a sudden close. Orloff was driven out of the house, charges of malfeasance were brought against him, and his banishment seemed certain.

But his mischance was the occasion of his good fortune. His adventure became known in the city and reached the ears of Catharine. She wanted to see the handsomest officer and was not long in bringing about a meeting. As it was difficult for any one to be brought unobserved into the palace she went in different disguises to Orloff's residence.

In a letter to Voltaire Catharine described Gregor Orloff as a "hero who deserved to be classed with the noblest Romans of the Republic." In a letter to a female friend she spoke of him as the "handsomest man of his time, one upon whom Nature has lavished gifts both of head and heart, possessed of knowledge, penetration, quick comprehension and a smooth address."

Catharine had already formed a project for getting rid of Peter and seizing the government. She communicated her plan to Orloff, who became her willing accomplice.

A number of officers were in the habit of assembling at Orloff's house to drink and carouse. They were good comrades and ready to render one another a service. For this reason Count Orloff was a lucky prize for Catharine.

He was not long in bringing over the officers to her side by painting the sufferings of the beautiful Grand Duchess and arousing on her behalf their enthusiasm and self-sacrificing devotion. Gregor's house, which had been a place of sensual orgies, now became a centre of revolution. How the revolution was conducted and its successful issue are familiar to history.

Soon after Peter's pusillanimous abdication and murder, initiated by Gregor and completed by Alexis Orloff, the Tzarina's favorite was openly proclaimed and formally established in the palace and beside the throne. After the example of the lovers of former Tzarinas he was provided with a numerous suite of apartments near those of the Empress, raised to the rank of count, presented with the highest orders and most lucrative employments, and for years enjoyed alone the privilege of wearing the portrait of the Empress at his button hole. It was set in an enormous brilliant, a "table diamond" in the form of a heart. It is needless to add that his wealth reached the sum of millions. The magnificent Stegelmann palace in St. Petersburg, afterwards the residence of Koscziusko, the estates and palaces of Gatschina and Ropscha, now owned by the Emperor Alexander, and numerous estates in Livonia, Esthonia and in the interior of Russia, became the property of Orloff. His power equalled that of a regent. He had the privilege of signing drafts upon the treasury to the amount of a hundred thousand rubles.

But all this did not content him. His ambition climbed still higher; he wanted to be not only the favorite of the Empress, but her husband, her lord, to be Emperor, and Catharine was so entirely under his influence that she consented to marry him and announced publicly her intention. But a number of her councilors opposed the adventurous project and it was finally abandoned. To indemnify Orloff she increased his revenues and conferred upon him the rank of Prince. But at last his pretensions grew intolerable. He publicly boasted of Catharine's indebtedness to him for her throne, and that it was in his power to dethrone her, and the Empress now began to look about her for a convenient opportunity to get rid of him.

In 1771 the pestilence broke out at Moscow and swept away a hundred and fifty thousand people. The Empress decided to send her favorite to that city with the hope of allaying the panic, not perhaps without the secret wish that he might never return. But Orloff took with him a skilful physician and returned safe to St. Petersburg after a successful visit. The Empress was compelled to feign great joy. She had a medal struck off representing Orloff as leaping like a second Curtius into the breach, and caused a marble momument to be erected after the Roman fashion at Zarskoje-Selo to commemorate his courageous visit to the pestilential city.

The Empress was now driven to look for another pretext for effecting Orloff's removal. She sent him to Fochschang, a small town in Wallachia on the confines of Moldavia, where a congress was sitting to conclude a peace with Turkey. His progress was that of a monarch. He was attended by marshals, chamberlains, pages, servants, and numerous equipages. His kitchen and wines were of the choicest, his vestments glittered with gold and silver. Catharine indulged the hope that his absence would be long. But a courier arriving with despatches from St. Petersburg brought the information that the Empress was amusing herself with other lovers during his absence. Orloff recognized the snare and without a moment's delay got into a simple kibitke and travelled day and night until he reached St. Petersburg.

The Court was informed of his return and

Catharine sent a messenger to meet him and offer him the palace of Gatschina as his residence.

Orloff was rendered desperate in the prospect of losing not his mistress but his power, and furious that he had permitted himself to be duped. He was a prisoner at Gatschina, where he consumed himself in unavailing rage. Meanwhile the Empress in her palace was scarcely less a prisoner than he. So great was her terror of him that it was difficult to quiet her alarm. "You do not know Orloff, he is capable of murdering me," she groaned incessantly. She had her door barred and ordered her groom of the chamber to keep incessant watch with a pistol.

The government at last decided to enter upon negotiations with the ex-favorite and endeavor to arrive at an agreement. But Orloff was immovable. He refused absolutely to resign his position as the Tzarina's lover. The latter attempted to propitiate him with the present of a million. He bluntly refused it.*

In spite of the fact that Orloff was unable to gain access to her and that he was strictly

---

*Brückner contents himself with remarking discreetly concerning this "crisis:" "It is impossible to furnish a particular account of it; it will suffice to say that the Empress made Orloff sensible of his disgrace." No, that is not enough.

guarded in his palace, the Empress lived in a state of perpetual terror. As a last resource she threatened him with imprisonment for life on his estate at Ropscha; but on the other hand, if he would yield and consent to resign his post of favorite, he would be suffered to retain his title with a yearly pension of a hundred and fifty thousand rubles, and to go wherever he pleased with the exception of St. Petersburg and Moscow. Again Orloff refused his consent to the offered terms and answered the threat of confinement at Ropscha with disdain.

An attempt was now made to pronounce him insane, and to place him in security. Yielding to force he suffered himself to be removed to the imperial pleasure palace of Zarskoje-Selo. Here he lived comfortably, assembling around him many of the most distinguished persons of the Residence-city. But one day he escaped while the guards were sleeping and with all secrecy made his way to St. Petersburg.

Catharine's terror when the dreaded Orloff appeared before her is not to be described. But the former favorite pardoned the "ungrateful" Empress and made his peace with her. He voluntarily relinquished his position of lover and was in return restored to all his dignities and received a yearly stipend of a hundred and fifty thousand rubles, six thousand serfs, a silver service made in France worth two hundred and fifty thousand rubles, and a marble palace which was afterwards acquired by the Government and made an imperial residence. In gratitude for the Tzarina's generosity he abated four hundred and sixty thousand of the millions, and purchased for her the enormous diamond which had made a part of the treasure of Nadir Shah and which is still the property of the Russian crown. He also devoted a portion of the money to the building of an arsenal at St. Petersburg.

But his peace of mind did not last. He had endeavored to console himself for the loss of his position as favorite but the contrast of his former power with his present insignificance weighed upon him. He tried to divert himself by travel, was now here, now there, passed a while at Moscow and then returned to St. Petersburg. At the latter place he married a young lady of the court named Ssinovieff, a relative of his mother. Catharine was delighted, and presented the bride of her former favorite with a gold toilet of inestimable value.

The young Princess Orloff was an excellent lady and exercised over her husband a great and favorable influence. But she did not long survive her marriage, and Orloff again plunged into a life of dissipation. He was soon after seized with a wasting disease which ended in insanity. He was haunted by visions in which he continually saw the bloody form of Peter the Third, and lived in a state of frenzied terror. But his sufferings did not last long. In April, 1783, the man who for twelve years had held the place of favorite to the exacting Catharine breathed his last. Contemporaries have not drawn a very unfavorable picture of his character. He possessed intelligence, courage, resolution, and goodness of heart, and showed himself, especially during the latter years of his life, to be a man of more than usual probity for Russia.

Catharine had by Orloff seven children. The best known of them was the son born in 1762, called Basil Gregojevitch, who received afterwards the sobriquet of Bobrinsky. He was startlingly like his mother in appearance, with the fierce and dissolute character of his father. Shortly after his birth he was placed in the charge of Schkurin, a stove-heater and later chamberlain and councilor, and was brought up by him until he entered the land cadet corps. The mask was then allowed to fall and it became an open secret that Basil Gregorjevitch was the son of the Empress and Orloff. The Empress gave him a million rubles, but imitating his prodigal father Bobrinsky threw his fortune into the streets, especially the streets of Paris. He was deprived of it in consequence and received instead a yearly pension of thirty thousand rubles. Paul I conferred on him the title of count.*

Another son of Orloff and the Empress was Galachtheon. He became an officer but died young in London in consequence of excessive dissipation. A third son died in childhood. Two daughters of Orloff and Catharine were brought up in St. Petersburg; one of them married Count Buxhövden, the other a Herr Klinger.

Orloff had at the time of his connection with the Empress† other affairs with ladies of the court. When Catharine discovered this she threw off all restraint. Alexis Orloff, a

---

*With reference to Bobrinsky see: Catharine's letters to him, Russ. Archives 1876. III. 13. Castera II. 35. Helbig, Russische Günstlinge 364. Bobrinsky's diary of the year 1779, Russian Archives 1877, III. 117. See Komarowsky's Memoirs in the "Eighteenth Century," I 393. 398. 401.

†He had a liaison with the Princess Dashkoff which antedated that with the Empress.

brother of Gregor, especially, was already in high favor on account of the part which he had taken in the revolution. He divided with Gregor the posts of dignity in the Empire. But a tranquil court life did not satisfy his ambition, and he obtained from the Empress the command of a fleet to be employed against the Turks. He was given the command of the Russian squadron in the Archipeligo and received dictatorial powers which rendered him unaccountable to authority and permitted him to employ the fleet in any undertaking he saw fit. The expedition proved nothing more than a showy comedy which cost a large sum and was altogether unprofitable. He made a few insignificant conquests which were restored to the Turks after the close of the war. Only one of his exploits gained him renown and consideration, or was celebrated by the Russians. This was the burning of the Turkish fleet at Tchefsme, in honor of which he received the name of Tchefsemenskoy. The vain victor took the utmost pains to hand down this achievement to posterity. The painter Philip Hackert was employed to portray the scene in accordance with Orloff's description from four different points of view. In order to bring the horrible spectacle forcibly before the eye of the painter the admiral caused a ship of war to be blown up in the harbor of Leghorn. The paintings, which succeeded admirably, are in the possession of the imperial house.

When Gregor Orloff lost his position of lover to the Empress the latter sent a messenger to Alexis Orloff forbidding him, also, to appear in St. Petersburg, and this order was not rescinded until years after, when she received the victorious admiral with tardy but all the more distinguished honors. At the theatres plays in verse were produced written expressly for his glorification in which Peter the Great and Catharine the Second figured. Medals were struck off representing him as the god of war, and at Zarskoje-Selo marble monuments were erected in memory of his "famous exploit," and—last, not least—enormous wealth was showered upon him.

But his day of glory was ended. Other stars were shining in the Empress's firmament of life and love. Orloff felt himself reduced to obscurity, and asked for his dismissal, which was cheerfully accorded him. He lived in retirement at Moscow until Paul ascended the throne and remembered him.

Soon after Paul's accession he summoned Count Alexis Orloff to St. Petersburg for the purpose of removing the remains of Peter the Third from the cloister of Alexander Newsky to the fortress. This was perhaps the most horrible day of Alexis Orloff's life. A few weeks later, he quitted Russia and did not return until after the murder of Paul. He died in Moscow in 1808, leaving a legitimate daughter and a natural son. The latter inherited his father's figure and his beauty, and was also for a short while accorded moments of intimacy by the now waning Catharine.

The two Orloffs brought their numerous brothers and cousins to the court. Ivan Gregorjevitch Orloff, the oldest of the brothers, became a subaltern in the guards, distinguished himself in the revolution of 1762, was made a count, and received large estates and the yearly pension of twenty thousand rubles allotted to all the leaders in the conspiracy. The fourth Orloff, Theodore, did not take a direct part in the revolution, but had nevertheless as an Orloff a good share in the prizes. Having distinguished himself in the Turkish war he was superabundantly feted and rewarded. He died at Moscow at the close of his ninetieth year. Vladimir Orloff, the youngest of the brothers, was educated at Leipsic, and upon his return the lad was made director of the

Academy of Sciences and chamberlain. Personally insignificant though he was, his revenues reached the sum of a hundred and thirty thousand rubles. Of the other four brothers Orloff little is known; they doubtless also fared well. The cousins and other relatives obtained good positions, but are not deserving of special notice.

The Orloffs, brothers and cousins, formed a splendid court of their own at St. Petersburg where they shone by reason of their beauty, their love of pleasure and the riches which the Empress showered upon them. They gave splendid entertainments and scattered treasures among the people with lavish hand. At no other court of the day was such prodigality to be witnessed.

During the reign of the brothers Orloff the lovers of Catharine were comparatively few and unimportant, but a recruit who came from a village to St. Petersburg whom she chanced to see pleased her so much that instead of placing him in a regiment she placed him in a livery. He was employed near her person until the affair came to the notice of Gregor Orloff, and the servant was made captain in a regiment. The Empress afterwards succeeded in bringing him back to the capital and gave him a high office in her household.

The affair of an officer named Wissensky did not prosper equally well. The Empress was so enamored of him for a time that it seemed as if the fortune of the obscure young officer might rival that of the Orloffs. But Wissensky's dream was short. He was abruptly dismissed and dispatched to a distant province.

Alexander Wassiltschkoff, a nobleman who was chosen by the Empress in 1772, retained his position longer. He remained twenty-two months by the side of the Empress, and was the most modest and disinterested of her lovers. He excited no malevolence, for he helped all and stood in the way of none. He made no large demands on his own account, nevertheless he received a hundred thousand rubles in specie, seven thousand serfs, sixty thousand rubles worth of diamonds, a silver service of the value of fifty thousand rubles, and a magnificent palace worth four hundred thousand rubles. He married and lived in Moscow the happiest husband in the world.

All of the Empresses of Russia had had lovers, but none raised the number of them so high as Catharine the Second. She changed them every twenty-four hours, or oftener. The position of a lover was a public office; the highest, most lucrative, and withal the most entertaining—at least so long as Catharine retained her beauty—which existed in Russia. The qualifications for the office were a handsome face, a fine figure, and above all great physical vigor.

The newly elected favorite was first made adjutant-general. This enabled him to attend the Empress everywhere without attracting observation. He occupied communicating apartments in the palace.

Shortly after his induction into office he received a hundred thousand rubles, and once every month he found twelve thousand upon his night table. The steward was charged with the duty of serving him with twenty-four covers, and of superintending his housekeeping. The favorite must not leave the house without the permission of the Empress. It goes without saying that he must not approach other ladies. The Empress, on the other hand, retained the right to have numerous transient lovers simultaneously with the declared favorite. Each as he fell out of favor was richly endowed and was ordered to travel and never to appear again in the presence of the Empress. This order only Potemkin disobeyed.

The Russian people and the government officials grew accustomed to this procedure. They came in time to regard it as natural that the Empress should divert herself with lovers after the severe cares of government, and the frequent changes were not viewed with displeasure. The example of the Orloffs had taught how dangerous a prolonged liaison might become. It was therefore always sought to provide her with insignificant persons and to fill their places very soon by others. But it happened that this supposed insignificance concealed such a genius as Potemkin.

Gregor Potemkin was born at Smolensk in 1736—according to some, at Warsaw in 1743—and received as the son of a retired officer a modest education. He was first destined for the church, but developing a military talent he was sent to St. Petersburg, and because of his fine figure was placed in a regiment of the mounted guards. On the accession of Peter the Third he became master of the watch, and was among those who were won over to the cause of the Empress. After the revolution he was made an officer and groom of the chamber, and was sent to Sweden to announce the accession of the new sovereign.

Upon his return he was one day employed

as a guide to the carriage of the Empress. When about to withdraw at the end of his service his horse became refractory and refused to move from the spot. The Empress looked up. The young officer was handsome, very handsome. She said: "Your horse is more cunning than you."

He understood the glance and wink, and a determination to become the favorite took root in his mind. At that time the brothers Orloff were at the height of their power, nevertheless Potemkin was not discouraged. He succeeded at an unguarded moment in obtaining access to the Empress, and was confounded by his good fortune. He vaunted it aloud, and boasted in the presence of Alexis Orloff of the favor he enjoyed. Orloff answered him disdainfully, angry words ensued, and Potemkin received a blow in the face which put out one of his eyes. The cause of the scandal became public, and the end was that Potemkin was sent, first to the army, and afterwards to his home. Here he lived for some time in sullen solitude, entertaining the idea of becoming a monk. Suddenly it occurred to him to write to Catharine, which he did, pouring forth his ardent love and longing, and begging to be received into favor.

The Empress, who meanwhile had got rid of the Orloffs, recalled him at once to the court. He now obtained a complete ascendency over her and used and abused it to the utmost. He made constantly increasing demands upon her, and after the example of Biron beat her if she dared to refuse him anything. Finally he, like his predecessor, aspired to her hand.

With this object in view, this greatest of roués suddenly became the most pious man in the capital. He denied himself his celebrated kitchen and lived on vegetables and water, confessed every day to the Empress's confessor, to whom he confided his intimate relations with the Empress and the uneasiness of his conscience which he could not reconcile to this illicit connection, imploring him to prevail upon her to consent to a consecrated union. The favorite supported his pious pleadings with glittering gold and deceitful promises.

The heart of the priest was not of stone, neither were his pockets sewed with a thousand threads. With tears in his eyes he conjured the Empress to abandon her life of sin and reconcile herself with God by a holy marriage bond. The shrewd, freethinking Catharine sent for Potemkin. With the tenderest accents she said :

"I love you; nevertheless, I am prepared to give you up sooner than imperil the salvation of your soul. If you cannot continue to be my lover without dreading the judgment of Heaven, go—I will take another."

The pious Potemkin was dismayed. He protested his willingness to forego marriage and retain his position as lover. But Catharine soon after supplied his place by others, and ordered him, according to custom, to travel.

Potemkin feigned to obey; but the following day he returned to the palace and seated himself unconcernedly in the presence of the Empress. She evinced no displeasure and retained him at the court.

Then began between Catharine and Potemkin a relation unique of its kind. Love is dead, live friendship. In the character of friend of the Empress, Potemkin became more powerful than ever, and, having lost her love, retained her unbounded confidence for the remainder of his life. It was he who provided her with new and ever new lovers, who as his creatures exerted themselves in his behalf so that his influence remained unshaken and after his liaison was at an end he continued still the most powerful man in the Russian Empire. The treasures lavished upon him were incalculable. His favorite amusement was to lie upon a couch and toss his jewels into the air with one hand, catching them with the other. This he called "playing cateract." At a dinner given in honor of his mistress, the Princess Dolgorouky, diamonds were served at dessert. He had a room furnished after an odd conceit of his own of which he always carried the key with him. It contained book shelves with numerous divisions as for a library. These were all well filled with volumes in quarto and octavo; but the leaves of these books consisted of bank notes.

Like Mentschikoff the favorite of Peter the Great and Catharine the First, he had his own court, with numerous officials and servants, which was not behind that of the Empress in brilliancy and prodigality. The profusion of his entertainments was beyond description. To procure melons or flowers for his mistresses, he sent couriers the distance of many hundred versts, to Astrakan or to Paris, to Poland or to Taurida. His dishes were of the rarest, his wines the most costly. The court chapel of the Prince provided the music, and in the pauses the most melodious songs were sung by the most beautiful songstresses. "Here," says an admirer of Potemkin who must have taken part in these fetes, "was found the only opportunity to see the Prince free from cares and in his most condescending moments; for although the majestic exaltation of Potemkin inspired every one with awe, he met each of his guests in the most condescending manner and without distinction."

At the close of the repast, which never lasted more than two or three hours, the Prince conversed with the guests, after which cards were played. The cards were not of gold but of precious stones. While the games were in progress all was still as in a chamber of death. There was nothing but playing; no one dared to speak.

Still more brilliant than his dinners were Potemkin's balls, which must have cost at least a hundred thousand rubles. Generals and diplomatists were invited from all quarters. In 1779, on the occasion of the birth of Paul's daughter Catharine, Potemkin prepared a great fete. He had splendid buildings and a dancing hall erected on his estate of Oserki on the Neva, and a floating temple on whose facade and spires sparkled the names of the members of the imperial family. Supper was served in a grotto the exact counterpart of a grotto in the Caucasian mountains, ornamented with laurels and roses and a painted waterfall. A choir sang songs in ancient Greek.

But all the previous fetes were cast into the shade by one given by him a short while before his death, on the 28th of April, 1791. Artists and artisans were busily employed in the house-decorations and new furnishings, gobelin tapestries and carpets were woven for the occasion; two hundred large lustres and the most costly mirrors were brought from the city and sixteen thousand pounds of wax for illuminating. The glass lanterns took the form of every variety of fruit and flower. Free tables were set for the populace, and garments and shoes were prepared for distribution at the moment the Empress appeared. From early morning the people were peering stealthily at the beautiful objects, but a rumor ran that any person who intruded before the appointed hour would be sent to the army, and they waited peacefully and quietly until their hour should come. Suddenly the news spread that the Empress had arrived. Then there was no waiting. No one wanted to be left in the lurch, and all rushed precipitately upon the viands and presents; hopeless confusion reigned, and not until force was used could the plunderers be dispersed.

This was a prelude. Gradually the guests

assembled; arriving last of all, the Empress. It is difficult to form a conception of the sumptuousness of this fete. Most splendid of all was the dancing room. Seventy-four couples in fancy costume opened the dance amid the singing of songs composed by Deschawin in praise of the Empress, and sung by invisible voices, the singers being concealed in secret galleries: "Mahomet is vanquished, the Don is in the hands of the Russians, from Ismael their dying groans have been heard. The Empress is like unto Minerva, Potemkin unto Mars, Alexander, the grandson of the Empress, may be likened to Alexander the Great, his brother to the great Constantine, the restorer of Byzantium. The might of ancient Rome and the radiance of Hellas are united under the sceptre of Russia."

The dances, which were original, were created after the design of Potemkin by the famous masters La Picq and Canziani, who received for the evening, respectively, six and five thousand rubles. Near a wonderful clock of peculiar mechanism and ingenious striking machinery, which cost forty thousand rubles, stood a Persian puppet on the back of an artificial elephant, and by striking on a bell invited the guests to witness a play. "The False Lovers," and a pantomime, " The Merchant of Smyrna," the latter representing a slave market, in which all the characters were slaves excepting—the free Russians!

Night came on. In the gardens all was ablaze. Fourteen thousand lamps and twenty thousand candles illuminated the scene. Innumerable fruit trees entranced the eye, but their fruits, so natural and delusive, were of glass. Artificial also was the softly shimmering turf, artificial the grottoes with mirrors which reflected everything a thousand fold. In the middle of the garden gushed a fountain of lavender water, and near it sparkled a pyramid of gold and precious stones, and these were real. Strange singing birds warbled in marvellous nests. In the sky-blue temple supported on marble columns stood a statue in marble of the Tzarina veiled in purple, in her hand a horn of plenty from which fell treasures of gold coin and costly orders, and underneath the inscription: "The Mother of the country, my Benefactor." Potemkin, wearing a frock of crimson red and a scarf of rare lace, a hat of precious stones so heavy that an adjutant was employed to sustain it, prostrated himself on the steps of the temple and repeated lines presumably of his composition: "Que puis-je t'offrir en hommage? Je suis moi-même ton ouvrage. Mon pouvoir et mon sort son sortis de ta main."

Upwards of thirty thousand persons were present at this fete, the cost of which must be reckoned by the hundred thousand. For candles alone seventy thousand rubles were expended. The Prince himself was the most hilarious person present. It was a common observation of his that for a man to be adequate to his destiny pleasures and enjoyment were as essential as food.

But it often happened that the caprice of the host occasioned disagreeable interruptions to these fetes. The Prince, but a moment ago in high spirits, would suddenly show the utmost ill humor. The most frequent cause of the ill humor of this "Exalted" person, as Potemkin was customarily styled, was given by his mistresses, who were recruited from among the most beautiful women of the time and naturally awakened at a public ball the admiration of others besides their lord. These frivolous ladies did not always show themselves indifferent to some one or other of the gay gentlemen who sued for their favor, or even perhaps bestowed a larger share of their affection upon him than upon their elderly proprietor. If this came to the notice of Potemkin he flew, in a rage, to the faithless one, tore off her head dress and turned her contemptuously out of doors. Sometimes he was so much enraged as to suspend the fete and dismiss his guests, but in the course of a few hours, repenting that he had made his whole company responsible for the sins of his faithless mistress he despatched messengers to recall them in haste and the ball would continue as before. That this was endured is an index of the epoch. From the omnipotent Potemkin everything was borne with patience. The magnates of the Empire crawled in the dust at his feet, even the successor to the throne trembled in his presence.

That he was an extraordinary man cannot be denied. Yet his rôle was one that could only have been played in Russia, and only in the Russia of Catharine the Second. In him were blended the most opposite qualities. By the side of his great prodigality grinned mockingly the extremest avarice. His despotism and hardness were equalled only by his arrogance and his ambition was only exceeded by his skill in the art of flattery. He squandered millions on his mistresses and remained in debt for beggarly trifles. No one was so superstitious and no one so crafty as he. He had great imaginations, and boldly launched forth into well nigh inconceivable enterprises. No hindrance deterred him from reaching his goal; but when reached, he lapsed into a state of lethargy and satiety, and did not avail himself of what he had won. He created for himself numerous offices and became a burden upon the country, yet he was indispensable to it, and when he died he left a void which could not be filled. He carried an enormous load upon his shoulders, such as no one but him could have borne; but he derived no satisfaction from his various employments, the ambition to reach out after something new robbed him of contentment and peace. All in him was disorder and unrest; his activity, his conduct, his character. Where he was, there was inquietude; to see him was to dread his caprices. He cared for few persons, and for these in his own way. Whoever flattered him was welcome; whoever contradicted him was his mortal enemy. He forgot the good that was done him, but he never forgot the evil. He promised much, but performed almost nothing.

No one, perhaps, has filled so high a place who possessed so little education, yet he had an extensive knowledge of all subjects. The want of study was compensated for by a keen perception, a quick comprehension, and a retentive memory. He conversed with equal ease with a scholar or an artist, a priest or an artisan. His whims were incredible. To-day he wanted to be Duke of Courland; to-morrow, King of Poland. Suddenly he determined to renounce the world and retire into a monastery, betook himself to penance and mortification, and twenty-four hours later he gave one of his most extravagant fêtes. To-day he wished to be a general; to-morrow, a statesman; again, a simple courtier, a private citizen, or all of these combined. He built costly palaces, and before they were ready for occupation he sold them. At times he remained for weeks in a cave with a girl, and could not be prevailed on to attend to his duties; then suddenly would appear before the throne decorated with the orders of every land, and insist upon the partition of Turkey; anon, after driving out in a carriage blazing with gold, would hold a reception at his residence barefooted, unkempt and unwashed.

He had singular good fortune in war because he had the skill to avail himself of superior ability. But here also his caprice came into play. The capture of Ismailoff by Suvaroff in 1790 was the result of a wager with a lady with whom he was in love and who visited him in his camp at Jassy. The conversation at table turning upon the siege of that place, she expressed her belief that it would be impossible to capture the stronghold. Potemkin answered: "Madam, I will engage that Ismailoff shall be in my hands in twice twenty-four hours." "But not without an enormous sacrifice of life." "That is a trifle. Russia has plenty of men." Potemkin won the wager, which cost the lives of twenty thousand brave men.

It was at Jassy that he established warehouses in order that the mistresses who accompanied him on his campaigns might have the opportunity to provide themselves with fine and fashionable clothing. It will be seen how he thought of everything.

In waste and desolate places he created towns, in order to deceive the Empress on her journeys as to the value of his conquests. His was the most inventive brain that ever conceived and deceived in Russia. He has been not inappropriately described as the reflected image of Russia. He was as overwhelming as the Empire; like it his mind and character were filled with fruitful fields beside desert wastes. In him were united the Asiatic and the European, the Slav and the Tartar, the medieval barbarian and the veneer-like culture of modern Half-Asia.

That he had enemies in abundance will be believed. They called him the "Prince of Darkness," and characterized him as the evil genius of his country. Once, when the Empress fell ill he surrounded his house with redoubts and bastions which he garrisoned with his most trusty followers, justly fearing for his life in the event of Catharine's death. But he had no cause; he died before her.

His death was no less strange than his life. For a year he had withdrawn from active part in affairs and abandoned himself to debauchery. Suddenly he roused himself and hastened off to the frontier. But before he reached the army he was seized with a violent attack of a disease which had long before been brought on by his excesses. Instead of exercising prudence he gave himself up to debauchery, his strength gave way, he sank on a country road and died an inglorious death in the presence of a few attendants, who had to drag him to the city in a cloak like any beggar.

Potemkin left a property which would have enriched a state. Besides bank notes of all the trading centers of Europe, amounting to untold millions, he possessed an incalculable treasure in diamonds, silver, gold and porcelain; he left also over three millions of debts. His heirs were five nieces and three nephews. To these, especially the former with all of whom he had held tender relations, he left large bequests. Each of them received twelve thousand Polish serfs, the nephews four thousand and a third of his personal estate.

When the news of his death reached Catharine it plunged her in despair. She had accustomed herself to look upon him as the stay of her throne; now she grew tremulous, tottered, fell ill and died.

"I have no one to lean upon; no one can fill Potemkin's place; he was never to be bought."

Count Esterhazy who resided at that time at the Russian court wrote to his wife: "Since the death of Potemkin everything here is plunged in gloom. The Empress has not once quitted the palace, there is not the the smallest court circle; she has not played cards in her room."

In her letters to Grimm the Empress described her grief at her loss: "My pupil, my friend, almost my idol, is dead," and she made over him the most enthusiastic epilogue. "La qualité la plus rare en lui était un courage de coeur, d'esprit et d'ame, qui le distinguait parfaitement du reste des humains, et ceci faisait que nous nous entendions parfaitement bien et laissions babiller les moins entendus a leur aise. Je regarde le Prince Potemkine comme un très-grand homme, qui n'a plus rempli la moitié de ce qui était a sa portée."

She had the most profound admiration for Potemkin's intellectual gifts, and could not dispense with his counsels, of which she felt herself in continual need. When he remained for years absent in the South she missed him terribly, and filled with anxious solicitude for his health besought him to spare himself, addressed him with all manner of pet names such as "little dove," "little soul," "my heart," "little father," "my angel," "papa," "dear grateful pupil." "Rest assured," she wrote in 1780, "that my friendsiip for you, my dearest, is equal to your attachment for me." At another time, "It is desolate without you. When you are not by me I seem to myself to be without hands." She describes him as "one of the drollest and most amusing originals of this age of iron." When in 1778 she ordered for him a service of of Sèvres porcelain she observes that it is "pour le premier rongeur de doigts de l'univers, pour mon cher et bien aimé Prince Potemkin, et pour qu'il soit plus beau, j'ai dit qu'il est pour moi." She cannot say enough in praise of his good looks. He, as well as Gregor Orloff, was "the handsomest man of his time." His amiability and his ideas she characterizes as inexhaustible, and praises even his good humor (so much for the point of view!) in extravagant terms. Finally she observes with modesty : "Il a plus d'esprit que moi et tout ce qu'il faisait était profondément réfléchi."

But he also understood how during a prolonged separation to keep alive her friendship by letters such as these : " Matuschka, rodnaja little mother, dear mother ; Most gracious Empress leave me not without news. Do you not then comprehend the measure of my attachment * * * in this state of uncertainty anxiety robs me of all my strength. I can neither sleep nor eat ; I am worse than a child. Necessary as it is to break up and go to Cherson I cannot make up my mind to stir. If my life has any value for you let me know at least this one thing—that you are well."

Yes, Potemkin had become all in all to the Empress, the prop of her throne, and her most skilful pander. When he was forced to vacate his post as lover he took care to provide for this important office a creature of his own, Peter Savadovsky.

Peter Savadovsky was the son of a Russian priest of the Ukraine. By his father's care he had received an education, that is to say instruction in latin, history and philosophy. He came first to St. Petersburg as a scribe in the house of Count Rasumovsky, was by the latter recommended to Count Rumjänzof who took him into his chancellery, and soon after turned him over to the Empress as her secretary. The Empress was much pleased with him and showed him marked favor over every one else, with great caution however, to avoid exciting the jealousy of Potemkin who was still her lover. But when Potemkin was obliged to retire, having remarked the direction in which the eyes of the Empress were turning he was cunning enough to propose Savadovsky as his successor, a proposition which was quite superfluous but which for appearance sake was accepted with thanks. This happened in November, 1764.

Savadovsky was installed in the apartment in the palace which Potemkin had occupied, and received, although he was still secretary, the title of major-general. He did not long retain his position. Attempting to undermine the omnipotent Potemkin and to drive him out of the head as well as the heart of the Empress he was himself dismissed. He remained however at the court, where he filled important positions and was the first after Potemkin who was permitted to reside near Catharine after having filled the office of lover. Potemkin looked around for a successor to Savadovsky wishing to anticipate the Empress and prevent a choice which might be displeasing to himself.

There was a serf residing at the court named Soritch, who was a protégé of his. This was the man. He possessed the requisite qualifications of beauty and strength, and he lacked intelligence and character, which suited Potemkin very well. He made Soritch his adjutant, and presented him to the Empress in the uniform, which set off his person well, of a lieutenant of hussars. Catharine was pleased with the selection, and on the appointed day Soritch was assigned to the appartments of a favorite and occupied them eleven months. In the matter of presents he was not less fortunate than his predecessors. A half million in money, twenty thousand rubles for his first establishment, eighty thousand for his establishment upon an estate, two hundred and forty thousand for the payment of his debts, and the stated monthly income of a favorite. Beside the specie he received fifteen hundred serfs and an estate in Livonia worth a hundred and twenty thousand rubles. Finding this still too little, Catharine added to it the crown revenues for ten years and the office of Commander of the Order of Malta for Poland, which yielded ten thousand rubles yearly. Finally the "munificent" sovereign presented her lover with the city and domain of Schklow, in Poland, which cost four hundred and fifty thousand rubles. To attempt to enumerate the favorite's treasure in diamonds would be a hopeless task. His shoulder straps, his hats, even his shoe buckles, consisted of diamonds and other precious stones. Who can say how much he might have cost the state had he not, like Sadavowsky, made the blunder of attempting to belittle Potemkin in the eyes of the Empress. Potemkin lost no time in representing to her that it was beneath the dignity of the most enlightened princess of her time, a friend of the greatest and most enlightened intellects in the world to permit a man so unlettered as Soritch near her. Catharine was astute enough to understand, but as she was always disposed for a change of lovers she suddenly discovered that Potemkin was right, and commissioned him to give Soritch a more worthy successor.

The court was at that time at Zarskoje-Selo. Soritch was in his chamber in a happy mood, playing with his diamond treasures, when the order of the Empress arrived to depart for his estates and not undertake to see her again. He was compelled to set out that same hour for Schklow, where the loss of his position as lover was well compensated for by the life of a prince. He lived with great prodigality, even supporting a theatre. This continued as long as Catharine lived and sent him continually fresh reinforcements; but at last the impure fountain dried up and he became embarrassed; was obliged to mortgage his estates and part with his treasures. At one time it had seemed as if his star was again in the ascendant. When a favorite, Mamonoff, threatened to become dangerous to Potemkin the latter lost no time in bringing about a meeting between Catharine and Soritch with the hope of overthrowing Mamonoff and reinstating the former favorite. Soritch was still handsome and vigorous, and pleased Catharine—but for one day only. He was again dismissed with presents and hurried back to Schklow, where he was still living in the time of Paul.

As a successor to Soritch, Potemkin presented to the Empress Korsakoff, a captain of cuirassiers; Bergmann, a Livonian, and a certain Ronzoff, a natural son of Count Voronzoff. After conversing with all three Catharine's choice fell upon Korsakoff, a guard in her ante-chamber whose good looks had attracted her attention. Handing him a bouquet, she said :

"Carry this to Prince Potemkin. I wish to speak to him."

Potemkin understood the hint. "As a reward to the bringer of an imperial present" he made the captain his adjutant, and the following day the Empress made him her own adjutant and assigned to him the apartments at Zarskoje-Selo which Soritch had occupied.

Korsakoff had, properly speaking, only changed his apartment. Formerly he had kept guard in the antechamber ; now he kept guard in the sleeping chamber. But he proved unfaithful. Catharine surprised him in her own sleeping apartment in the arms of the pretty Lady Bruce, one of her ladies in waiting. In the first moment she was struck dumb at this effrontery, then she laughed, the noble Empress, and—took another. The Countess Bruce was permanently banished from the Court, and Korsakoff, who had received property and presents to the value of a million, and now as a parting present received a hundred and seventy thousand rubles, followed her, but soon after quitted her and lived with the Countess Stronganoff-Trubetskoy.

The great good fortune which attended the favorites turned the heads of many persons. The ministerial secretary, Ivan Strachoff, an uncultured, ill-favored little personage of uncouth manners whom the Empress on one occasion had addressed graciously, conceived from that moment the idea of becoming the favorite. He continually thrust himself upon Catharine's path and sought to attract her attention. He succeeded, and thereby procured her much amusement. Finding herself alone with him, she determined to amuse herself with his popinjay notion of captivating her favor. She said to him good-humoredly:

"Ivan Strachoff, ask for something that you wish."

The fellow sank on his knees and cried out with all the strength of love:

"Your love, Your Majesty!"

This was too much. He was not permitted

again in her presence. But a man who loved her so much must not be unhappy, and Catharine sent Strachoff presents in money, serfs and land, with the high order of Vladimir, and made him vice governor of Kostrona. So Ivan Strachoff had also his share of a favorite's luck and without the exacting duties attendant upon it.

Alexander Lanskoi was a nobleman of good family, and served in the Chevalier Guard. He became known to the Empress while Korsakoff was still in favor, and received then an appointment as her next "adjutant-general." Being at the time in delicate health and often indisposed, he was engaged in advance and given the sum of ten thousand rubles for his entertainment. Lanskoi entered into relations with Potemkin, and placed himself under his protection. This proved of service to him. Potemkin kept Lanskoi with him for a few months, and during Holy Week, 1780, he reminded the Empress of him, and her health being now restored he entered upon his office. In a short while he won a great empire over Catharine although affecting to feel himself insignificant and without influence, and would have trumped them all but for his sudden death in 1784 at the age of twenty-seven. He was unequal to his position, and the expedients which she had him resort to ended by destroying him.

The Tzarina now, as so often before when a lover was torn from her against her will, was plunged in despair and dissolved in tears and lamentations. She remained shut up in her chamber all day, would see no one, hear nothing; paid no attention to the government or to the country, arraigned herself, arraigned Heaven, wanted to abdicate, wanted to die, and put on mourning like a bereaved widow.

Her only consolation was in the society of a sister of Lanskoi's who strongly resembled him. In this time of deep sorrow and despondency she wrote to Grimm; "My happiness has departed. I shall not outlive this grief. I had hoped that my young friend would be the staff of my old age." She extolled his capacity, his development, his improvement in knowledge and taste. She had brought him up, he was grateful and gentle, and shared with her everything. "My sitting room, which I so loved," she concludes, "seems to me an empty cave, where I wander as a ghost; I am so agitated I can see no one, and continually break forth in sobs; I cannot sleep or eat; reading wearies me, I have not the strength to write, and do not know what is to become of me. I know only that in my whole life I have never been so unhappy as since my dear friend left me."

Catharine's enthusiasm for Lanskoi was not generally shared. He gave himself little concern about public affairs, but was an object of universal fear. Joseph II. sued for his favor, as did Frederick William II. and Gustavus III., but he repulsed them all, so great did he feel himself. It was a blessing to Russia when he died. His cupidity was insatiable. He left behind him in money alone more than seven millions, not to speak of the many millions represented by his collection of pictures and medals and his landed estates. Yet with all this wealth he was so avaricious that he shamefully permitted his nearest relatives to starve. He bequeathed his possessions to the Empress, who, however, "munificently" gave all to his relatives, buying at a high price his collections and silver plate—to be presented to another favorite.

Lanskoi was buried in the garden of Zarskoje-Selo, and the Empress erected over his grave a simple but costly monument. One night the grave was dug up, the coffin broken open and the corpse defaced and covered with abusive inscriptions. After this Catharine caused them to be placed in a separate mausoleum.

When Lanskoi died Catharine swore: "Lanskoi is the last. Never again shall a man's lips touch mine or a man's heart beat on mine." She swore it devoutly and solemnly, for she believed herself about to die; but she continued to live, and life had claims upon her—tremendous claims.

More than a year passed after Lanskoi's death, and, with the exception of a few trifling infractions of her vow, Catharine courageously withstood everything masculine. Then came the reaction.

She cast her eyes about for a new adjutant-general. The Princess Dashkoff offered her son, a handsome young officer. After an interview the Empress found that she liked him, but Potemkin was fearful of Dashkoff's influence and succeeded in obtaining the dismissal of the candidate.

In his place he proposed a young subaltern of twenty-two, Alexander Jermoloff, who found favor notwithstanding his fair complexion—Catharine did not like fair men—and that he had an ugly, flat nose. But the long interval since Lanskoi was unbearable, and, in her haste to make good the loss of time as fast and as fully as possible, she did not as before demand good looks but took whatever came in her way, and thus took Jermoloff, who was ugly and unprepossessing.

Jermoloff was a distinguished man and well liked. He helped whom he could, was as upright as a man in his day could be, and spoke the truth when it was necessary. The last-named virtue was the cause of his disgrace. He exposed some irregularities of Potemkin's, and upon the Empress reproaching the latter with them, the Prince said :

"I see whence come these complaints. Your white Moor—for so he called Jermoloff, on account of his light hair and flat nose—your white Moor tells you all that. You can choose between him and me."

Catharine chose, and Jermoloff was dismissed.

Jermoloff who relatively received few presents (in sixteen months about five hundred thousand rubles), was succeeded by Alexander Mamonoff, lieutenant-captain of the guard. He, too, owed his place to Potemkin, who extolled the young man to the Empress and arranged to send her a picture by him. Her criticism of the picture was to be understood as expressive of her intentions toward the bringer. Catharine did not look at the picture, she saw only the bearer, and remarked: "Tell the Prince it is a good picture, but I do not like the coloring; in other words, it is good-sized but has an ugly face."

But in spite of the bad coloring Mamonoff was chosen and became a personage of importance. Next to Potemkin, he was the most gifted of her lovers. Of course she extolled him: "He is an angel, an invaluable man, and becomes every day more worthy to be loved." He had musical talent, artistic taste, and many-sided culture. But he had one defect. The elderly Empress did not content him. He formed a relation with a Countess Skawronska, a niece of Potemkin's. This was pardoned him and he made good his fault by increased zeal, renounced the Countess Skawronska, and—formed a new connection with the Princess Schtscherbatoff. Catharine heard of it and almost died of jealousy. To be certain, she summoned Mamonoff and said to him: "I am old, and feel that your future ought to be provided for. I will give you a wife who is both rich and distinguished."

Mamonoff then confessed his relations with the Princess Schtscherbatoff.

"It is true, then," exclaimed Catharine,

scarcely able to stand. Jealousy and mortified pride were raging furiously within her, nevertheless she commanded herself, and—shall we say nobly?—permitted the young man to go unpunished. With a few expressions of her dissatisfaction to her circle, the unpleasant affair was dismissed. "No one can imagine what I suffer," she said to some of her intimate friends; "if only he had not so long kept silence, leaving me in the dark. But God be with them; may they be happy." She expressed more anger in a letter to Potemkin, who months before had made up his mind to displace this favorite. She now saw that he had been entirely right. "I have received a bitter lesson," she wrote, "but I put an end to the farce as soon as possible." To keep up appearances and not give rise to gossip, she paid the wedding expenses and made the bridal pair handsome presents. In foreign circles it was declared that the Empress had been almost frenzied.

Mamonoff was more practical than his predecessor, Jermoloff. On the day of his induction into office he received sixty thousand rubles in addition to the revenues proceeding from his numerous titles and dignities. On each of his birthdays and baptism days (he was favorite from 1787 to 1789) the Empress gave him a hundred thousand rubles, and on several different occasions over a million. To this must be added his estates, which yielded sixty-three thousand rubles, the hire of twenty-seven hundred serfs which he had in Nischny-Nofgorod, and his treasures in precious stones.

Catharine's amours ended with a platonic love. Her last lover was named Plato Suboff.

Plato Suboff was the son of a rich man who held a high official position, but had not much education. At twenty-two he served in the horse guards, and was promptly chosen to fill the breach which Mamonoff's sudden exit had created. He was the only favorite who succeeded Potemkin whom the latter had not chosen. Potemkin was at the time absent from the capital and the case was urgent. As Mamonoff had by an exception to a general rule retained his apartments up to the time of his marriage, the Empress vacated some of her own rooms for the new comer. It astonished no one when the next day an unknown young man was seen arm in arm with the fat old Empress — a tender pair. He walked with covered head while behind him waddled all the magnates of the Empire, vying with each other for a gracious glance from the boy who yesterday had waited humbly in their antechambers.

Suboff was not content with the position of lover; he wanted political significance also, and he acquired it fast enough. It was his voice that soon decided the most weighty affairs, and he would have doubtless superseded Potemkin had the latter been still alive.

Suboff accumulated vast riches. On the first day he received thirty thousand rubles for his establishment, and the revenues from his estates amounted to over two hundred thousand. He was the last official favorite. When Catharine, whose body was already in a state of corruption, with a terrible shriek bade adieu to life, Suboff was adroit enough to be the first to salute the new monarch. Paul said to him graciously: "My mother's friend, be mine also." For a time their relations were friendly; but Paul's caprices were very changeful, and when one day he made the discovery that eighteen thousand rubles were missing from the artillery fund which was in the hands of Suboff he dispossessed him of all his functions. Suboff quitted the country, but he returned before long and revenged himself on Paul. He was one of the arch conspirators in the murder of the Tzar in 1801.

Suboff was not yet twenty-five when Catharine, aged sixty, selected him as her lover-consort. She treated him not only as lover but as son, cared for his education and was so enamored of her work that he became her idol, and—if any one may so speak in such a case—the best loved of her lovers. She lauded him, like all the rest, in her letters to Grimm: "Suboff is industrious, has an excellent disposition and a most admirable quality of mind; he is a man whom you will hear of. I have it in my power to make of him another factotum."

But he had the same defect as Lanskoi. She brought therefore to his support his brother Valerian, who was younger and stronger than Plato, and the handsome and vigorous Peter Ssaltykoff. With these three the aged expiring Catharine led a life the most horrible and shameful that ever was in the history of the world. She formed a secret society composed of her favorites, her most trusted courtiers and court ladies, whom she assembled twice a week under the name of the "little hermitage," at a house set apart for the purpose. All of them wore masks, and under the protection of masks everything was permissible. There were obscene dances and plays, and a perfect saturnalia was held.

Meanwhile the best men of the land shed their blood on the field of battle for the Empress and her fame, in Sweden and in Turkey; for such a woman Poland was conquered and wiped out, and while she expended millions upon her orgies and her favorites, the gaunt arms of famine clasped in tight embrace the suffering and enslaved Russian people.

Fortunately the end was drawing near. The diseased and pest-stricken Empress could not much longer hold out.

At the age of sixty-seven Catharine still possessed the remains of beauty. She wore her hair always arranged with antique simplicity and in a tasteful style of her own. She was of medium height and very corpulent. It was said that no other woman of her size could have dressed with so much taste and grace. A contemporary has thus described her: "Her vivacity and familiarity in private circles seemed to immortalize youth and gayety in her neighborhood. Those who had access to her and were present at her toilets were enchanted with her affability and condescension; but as soon as she had put on her gloves to quit her chamber and appear in public in the other apartments, she at once assumed a totally different bearing and appearance. The amiable, sprightly woman gave place to the grave and majestic Empress. A person seeing her then for the first time would not have found her below the conception he had formed of her. He would have said, yes, that is she; the Semiramis of the North. To her as little as to Frederick II. could the maxim be applied: *Praesentis minuit famam.*

"She walked slowly and with short steps. Her brow was serene, her regard tranquil and often cast down. She saluted with a slight inclination that was not without grace, but with an artificial smile that came and went with the bow. When she offered her hand to a stranger to kiss she did so with much graciousness, generally asking a few questions as to his arrival in St. Petersburg and his travels. She had no sooner spoken than the artificial harmony was dispelled, and one saw only the empty mouth and sinking, ravaged cheeks. Her voice was inarticulate and hoarse, the lower part of her face assumed as she spoke a coarse and repulsive expression, and the eyes, when they forgot their rôle, were false, while a wrinkle on the bridge of the nose completed the whole." *

---

* At this period a portrait of her was made by the painter Lampi. It was very flattering, but the wrinkle on the bridge of the nose was visible. When Catharine

In her latter days Catharine greatly deteriorated physically. The once beautiful woman was not only altered and ugly from excessive dissipation, she became a mere unappetising lump of flesh and clothes. She ascended the stairs with so much difficulty that she had to be assisted, almost carried, and her steps were so painful that the entrance to her palace was covered over and over with the softest carpet. She was perfectly shapeless, her legs were swollen and covered with offensive sores, and the odor which exhaled from her person was intolerable. To disguise it she expended a small fortune in perfumery, which she had poured over her from morning till night and from night till morning. A former corsair, Lambrono-Cazzioni, whom Admiral Ribas brought to St. Petersburg, and who played the part of court fool, offered her a remedy for this unpleasantness: washing her feet in cold sea water. He washed them for her as often as possible, for which he was well remunerated, but which naturally produced no effect. The evil grew worse and worse, and resulted gradually in a state of living putrefaction. At last,

---

saw it she was very angry and had the picture painted over. This time she came forth as a blooming woman such as she had been in her best days.

in November, 1796, after she had notwithstanding her threatening condition passed the morning gayly with her lover, she broke down and expired in a long death struggle to the great joy of Paul, whom she hated, and who certainly cherished no deep affection for his mother.

Attempt has been made to throw a veil over the immorality of Catharine by the assertion that a great nature like hers could not be strictly held to the traditional standards of civic morality.

A pretty deviation that!

And in what did Catharine's heaven-storming greatness consist?

It cannot be denied that she is in a measure entitled to be styled "the Great," if that epithet be used to characterize an epoch; but it should not be overlooked to how great an extent her military successes were the result of chance, while within despotism and destruction prevailed as completely as in the worst days of former centuries. Every general, every governor, was a despot who extorted and oppressed at his will. Honors, justice, even the distinctions of learning, were publicly sold to persons destitute of education or character, honor or merit. And the system of favorites!

It is needless here to recur to this condition of moral anarchy. The portraits which have been unfolded in miniature will speak for themselves and need no commentary. The sums thus incidentally estimated, wrung from the people in order that inferior men whose only merit consisted in their physical strength, or perhaps in a handsome person, might dissipate millions— not always in their own country—in revel and riot; the wealth of the government, the wealth of the people, regarded as a lawful booty; the refuse of the Empire lying on the steps of the throne, calling themselves ministers, marshals, generals, counts, princes, and enveloped in clouds of incense—truly a people who could suffer all this deserved nothing better.

At the court the most unheard of prodigality prevailed. Each favorite sought to outdo the others. Not only were the women like diamond-bedecked idols, but also the men. The fetes were such as could have been witnessed at no other court. Never before were seen such rich table decorations in gold and silver, porcelain, alabaster and porphory as at a fete given by Count Scheremetjeff in Moscow in 1787. At another given by Besborodkos, who habitually drove through the streets of St. Petersburg in a gold carriage, there were pyramids of gold and silver several yards high and broad. At another was played a game of chance for which piles of gold and diamonds were placed at the disposition of the guests; not to mention the already described luxe of Potemkin! Catharine herself was not behind her favorites and courtiers. She built for herself fairy palaces with entrancing gardens, and her journey to the Crimea swallowed up over ten million rubles.

All these are shadows which destroy the light that surrounds Catharine's reign as a glow-worm is lost in the darkness of an impenetrable night. What are her institutions, her monuments, her military achievements, beside the wounds her system of favorites inflicted on the life of the state—wounds from which the Empire still bleeds! Her excesses were only equalled by her thirst for fame, say rather by her inordinate vanity. Out of vanity she founded libraries and collections of art,—not out of any genuine enthusiasm for art or learning. Only those great and celebrated men were encouraged and rewarded who grossly flattered her; but no talent, no genius, which blossomed in the shade was discovered and protected by her. She was jealous of the fame of other princes, and whatever attracted notice, she wished to have it also.* Her vanity made of her an authoress. The questionable literary renown of Frederick the Second allowed her no peace. *Anch' io sono pittore!* So she rushed into literature with a whole host of wretched plays, and an introduction to the Code of Civil laws, which she took bodily from Montesquieu and Beccaria.†

---

*The eagerness of Catharine to undertake enterprises which were never consummated, gave rise to an admirable witticism on the part of Joseph II. Three hundred cities which were said to have been founded by her, were in reality abandoned in the first stage of building. When Joseph II visited Catharine at Taurida she invited him to lay the second foundation stone of Jekaterinoslaw, of which she had just laid the first. Joseph afterwards declared that he and Catharine had entirely alone and in one day accomplished a great work. They had laid the first stone of a new city—and the last.

†Of the plays which Catharine wrote in the Russian language and in the composition of which her secretary Dershawin was—shall we say her collaborator?—the most interesting was a "historical representation," *Oleg*. It was a collection of scenes from tragedies, comedies, spectacular exhibitions and even operas and ballets. It was produced on the occassion of the peace with Turkey, and it was no trifling affair as seven hundred (say seven hundred) persons were engaged in it. The subject matter is drawn from Russian history, of which it represents a whole epoch. In the first act Oleg lays the foundations of Moscow; in the second he is at Kief where he marries his ward Igor and places him upon the throne. Here the old marriage ceremonials of the Tzars

Catharine made no concealment that in matters of love she thought more freely than any one else in the world. Ten years after her first romantic essay she said, not apologetically but philosophically: "I pleased; therefore the first half of the path of temptation had been travelled, and in such a case it is in human nature that the other half shall not be found wanting, for tempting and being tempted lie very close together, and in spite of the inculcation of the most beautiful morality in the soul

are skilfully blended with the national dances. After this Oleg sets out on an expedition against the Greeks. He is seen marching by with his army, and taking ship. In the third act he is at Constantinople. The Emperor Leo has agreed to a truce and has received him with great friendliness. While the two princes are together at table a chorus of young Greeks of both sexes recite songs in praise of Oleg, and dance before him some of the dances of ancient Greece. The Olympian Games are then performed upon a hippodrome. Next, a theatre appears out of the depths, on which are performed plays from Euripides in Greek costumes. At last Oleg takes his leave of the Emperor and hangs his shield on a pillar as a token that he has been in Constantinople and as a challenge to his successors to follow his example. That Catharine did not take literature seriously is shown by the following circumstance. While she was writing plays and pursuing literary fame, she deprived an ambassador at the court of Turin of his office simply and solely because he had written a tragedy and occupied himself with letters —or was it college rivalry?

as soon as the senses are stirred and show that they are, one is much farther advanced than one knows, and I do not know how the temptation can be prevented from becoming apparent. Flight, and flight alone, may do much, but there are cases, situations and circumstances, in which flight is impossible. How, in the midst of a court, can one fly, or avoid, or turn one's back? And without this refuge there can be nothing more difficult than to forego that which pleases one. Anything to the contrary is mere prudery, which was not implanted in the human heart, and no one carries his heart in his hand, so that he can by opening or closing it, stifle it or allow it to live."

While Catharine was still alive a number of satires upon her were written, painted, and engraved. Among the latter was one which was widely disseminated in Poland, of whose freedom she was the destroyer. It is entitled: "Catharine's wedding feast." She is sitting at table. On one side are Cossacks offering her the bloody limbs of Swedes, Poles and Turks; on the other are placed a row of naked young men like casks in a wine cellar, while an old woman presses the sap from the living casks and hands it to the Empress to drink in a bumper. Underneath are some rude lines.

See: The works on Peter the Third and Paul. Also, Mémoires de l'Impératrice Catharine II. London 1859. Memoirs of the Princess Dashkoff, London 1840 (German, Hamburg 1857. French, in the Russian-Polish Library, Paris 1860). Neuverändertes Russland oder Leben Katharinas der Zweiten. 1771-1772. Münnich, Mémoires Ebauche pour donner une idée de la sorte du gouvernement de l'Empire de Russie, 1774, Denkwürdigkeiten der Regierung Katharinas II. 1780. Coxe, Reise durch Polen, Russland. Zürich 1785. Catharina IIe, dargestellt in ihren Werken zur Beherzigung der Völker Europas. Berlin 1794. Katharina II., Abriss ihres Lebens und ihrer Regierung, Berlin 1797. Tannenberg, Leben Catharinas II. Leipzig, 1797. Uber das Leben und den Character der Kaiserin von Russland. Mit Freymüthigkeit und Unpartheylichkeit. Altona 1797. (Von Seume). Katharina II., Ein historischer Versuch. Im historisch-genealogischen Kalender für 1798, Berlin. Castera, Histoire de Catherine IIe. Paris 1799. Vie de Cathérine IIe, Paris 1798. Levesque, Histoire de Russie. Hambourg 1800. Masson de Blamont, Mémoires sécrètes sur la Russie et particulièrement sur la fin du Règne de Catherine IIe. et le commencement de celui de Paul Ier, Amsterdam et Paris 1800-1803. Georgi, Bemerkungungen auf eine Reise im Russischen Reich, St. Petersburg 1775. Pallas, Reise durch Russland 1771-1776. J. H. C. Meyer, Briefe über Russland, Göttingen 1778. Arndt's Petersburger Journal, 1776-1785. Johann Heinrich Busse, Journal von Russland, Petersburg 1794-1796. Magazin für die neue Historie und Geographie, 1767 ff. Heinrich von Reimers, St. Petersburg am Ende seines ersten Jahrhunderts, Petersburg 1802. Storch, Gemählde des russischen Reiches 1797-1803. Catharina II., Kaiserin von Russland Chemnitz, 1804. N. Karamsin, Lobrede auf Katharina II., Riga 1802. La Vaux, Histoire sècréte des amours de Catharine IIe. Alexandre Prince de G.,

Catherine IIe de Russie et ses favoris, Wurzburg. Abbé Georgel, Voyage a St. Pétersburg en 1799-1800, Paris 1818. F. W. Borck, Peter Paulowitch Semanows merkwürdige Begebenheiten während der Regierung Katharinas der Zweiten, Berlin 1834. Madame la duchesse d'Abrantès, Catharine IIe, Paris, 1835. Lettre d'un Russe a un Russe, simple réponse au pamphlet de Madame la Duchesse d'Abrantès, Paris 1835. Notizie dei regni di Caterina II. e Paolo I., 1839. (Prince de Ligne) La Cour de Russie il y a cent ans, de 1725-1783, Berlin 1858. Prince de Ligne, Portrait de S. M. Catherine IIe, Dresde 1797. Schlözer, Katharine II. und Friedrich der Grosse, Berlin 1859. Jauffret, Cathérine IIe, Paris 1860. Capefigue, La grande Cathérine, Paris 1862. Hermann, Geschichte des russischen Staates, V-VII. Ustrjaloff, History of Russia. Ssolowjef, History of Russia. Ségur Mèmoires ou souvenirs et anecdotes, Paris 1827. Mémoires du Prince de Ligne, Bruxelles 1860. Sabathier de Cabres, Cathérine IIe, sa cour et la Russie, 1772. Lebrun, Memoires, Paris 1870. Schtscherbatoff, Sittenverderbniss in Russland. Arneth, Joseph II. und Katharina II., Wien 1869. Karl Hillebrand, in the Deutschen Rundschau XXV, 388. J. Grot, Uber Katharinas Jugend, in the Russian Magazine "Old and New Russia," 1875, I. 122. Kutlebitzky, in the Russian Archives 1868, 8 and 9. Sablukoff's Memoirs in Frazer's Magazine 1865, VIII and IX. Memoirs of Prince Nikolay Wassiljewitsch Repnin (Potemkin's rival) in the Russian Archives 1869, 3. A, A. Baschilof describes court life under Catharine in the "Sara" 1871, and in the New Year's Almanac, Moscow 1850. Lubänowsky's Memoirs in the Russian Archives 1872. Dmitrijef, A Glance at my Life, Moscow 1866. Komarofsky, Memoirs, in the Russian Archives 1867, 2, 4, 5, 6, 10. Komarofsky the XVIII. Century, Moscow 1868. Siebigk, Brautfart Katharina II., Dessau 1875. A. Brückner, Katharina II. Berlin 1883. W. Vogt,

Vortrag über Katharina II., in the "Sammler" of the Augsburger Abendzeitung of 19th February, 1890. Crusenstolpe, Der russische Hof. Helbig, Russische Günstlinge. Sclösser, Geschichte des XVIII. Jahrhunderts. Golowin, Russische Geheimnisse. Leben Potemkins (by Helbig) in the "Minerva," 1798. Vie du prince Potemkin, par Cérenville, Paris, 1808. Lewschin, Life of Potemkin, Petersburg, 1811. Anecdoten zur Lebensgeschichte Potemkins, Freistadt am Rhein 1792. Letters from Catharine II to Potemkin in the Russian Archives 1870, 2 and 3. Papers of Prince Potemkin in the Russian Archives 1865. On the subject of Potemkin's feast see the letters of an unknown person in the Russian Archives 1866, 3. Chrapowitzky' Journal in the "Tschenija" of the Moscow society of history and antiquity, 1862. On the subject of Potemkin see, further, Moskwitjänin 1852, 3; Russian Archives 1867, 657-694; Baltische Monatsschrift 1870, XIX, 501-532, von Brückner; Samoilof, Biography of Potemkin, in the Russian Archives, 1867. 1011. Nadeshdin, Fürst Potemkin in the Russian Odessa Almanac for 1839, 76; Kolotof, Deeds of Catharine the Second, Petersburg 1811, vol. IV. Bantysch-Kamensky, Russian Generals, Moscow 1836, IV. A. Brückner, Potemkin, St. Petersburg 1891, (Russian). Karabanof, Gregor Orlof, Russkaja Starina V. 139. Barssukof, Gregor Orlof, Russian Archives 1873, 50-58. Biography of Suboff, Russkaja Starina XVI and XVII. Jacob Paul Lacroix, Deux lettres inédites de Cathérine IIe a Stanislaus Poniatowsky, Paris 1873. Letters of Catharine to Count Tschernytscheff, Russian Archives, 1881. The latest is Bilbassoff, History of Catharine II; German by Pezold, Berlin 1891, Bd. I und II. The continuation of which was forbidden this work in Russia, was published in Germany by Siegfried Cronback, Berlin 1892.

EPISODES FROM THE LIFE OF PAUL THE ECCENTRIC.

The Childhood of Paul.—The Experiment with the Countess Czartoryska.—His First Marriage to Wilhelmine of Hesse-Darmstadt.—His Wife's Affair with Count Andreas Rasumofsky.—Paul's Second Marriage to Sophia Dorothea of Württemberg.—Paul as Tzar.—His Erratic Behavior.—The Married Life of the Imperial Pair.—Character of the Empress.—The Mistress Nelidoff.—The favorite Kutaisow.—The Mistress Lopuchin.—The Murder of Paul.

COMPARISONS have often been drawn between Paul and his reputed father, Peter the Foolish. It is certain that he was as crack-brained, if not more so, than the latter. His childhood during the life time of Peter was not happy. The "father" well knew that his successor was not his own son* and had fully made up his mind to repudiate his faithless

---

* It has been asserted, but without foundation, that Catharine's child was a girl, and that Paul was a supposititious Finnlander.

consort and her bastard child, before Catharine forestalled him and ascended the throne of her son. As Paul advanced in years she had no disposition to relinquish to him the power she had learned to love so well and he was too weak to dispossess her by force.

But for fear her son might one day demand his rights she sought to enfeeble his mind by treating him like a slave, and she succeeded even beyond her intention.

In his childhood Paul gave evidence of the possession of good traits. He was sagacious, open hearted, good humored, quiet, and industrious. But these good qualities were perverted or destroyed, not through neglect only, but through actual suppression. The sagacity changed to deceitfulness, the franknesss to taciturnity, the good humor to a gloomy severity and a tyrannical and teasing disposition took the place of his peaceableness and industry. The Grand Duke was one of the most enslaved persons in all the enslaved Russia of Catharine the Second. Every lackey of a favorite of his mother had more freedom and more pleasure than he, her son, the rightful ruler of the Empire. He grew up thus a sacrifice to unhappy family relations, like the Tzarevitch

Alexis, like Peter the Foolish, and like them he also was destined to a violent death.

Catharine had already contemplated giving a wife to the heir to the throne, but he seemed of so cold a temperament and so physically weak that she feared he was not ripe for marriage. To acquire certainty on this point she employed the young Countess Sophia Ossipovna Czartoryska to test the question. The experiment proved successful. In due time the Countess gave birth to a son who was as much like Paul as a son could be like a father.* Having thus given so satisfactory proof of maturity Catharine no longer hesitated to marry him. But in choosing a wife for the successor to the throne it was important to select a princess who would not be dangerous to herself. She fixed her eyes upon the three daughters of the Landgrave of Hesse-Darmstadt and invited the Landgravine and her daughters to visit St. Petersburg. Her choice fell upon the Princess Wilhelmine, who appeared to her the gentlest and most harmless. The Princess united with the orthodox church, receiving the name of

---

*The boy was named Simeon Welikoy and was brought up by the Empress. When he was grown he entered the Marine. The Countess married Gregor Rasumofsky.

Natalia Alexejewna, and in 1773 was married to the Grand Duke.

The marriage was not especially happy, and the gentle princess proved to be still but deep water.

The Grand Duke had a friend, Andreas Rasumofsky, with whom he had been brought up, who was his constant associate and who possessed his entire confidence. The Empress observed that intimate relations subsisted between Rasumofsky and the Grand Duchess, and, naturally, the discovery enraged Catharine as such discoveries had always enraged the severely virtuous Elizabeth. She warned her son, and Paul detected an interesting correspondence between his wife and his friend. But before he had time to avenge himself the Grand Duchess died, in her first week of child bed. It was whispered that her death had been accelerated by Catharine. To avoid an open scandal, Rasumofsky was simply sent as ambassador to Venice and Naples.

For a few days Catharine feigned deep distress at the death of Natalia Alexejewna, then she began to busy herself with a new project of marriage. Prince Henry of Prussia brother of Frederick the Great who was then at St. Petersburg, proposed a marriage of the Grand

Duke with his niece the Princess Sophia Dorothea of Württemberg.

The Princess Sophia Dorothea was already betrothed to the hereditary Prince of Hesse-Darmstadt, but Prince Henry did not doubt that the great Empire of Russia would be of more worth in the eyes of the Princess than the little principality of Hesse-Darmstadt, and took upon himself to bring about a dissolution of the contract and the marriage of the Princess to the Grand Duke.

He despatched a courier to his brother, and the great Frederick himself became the mediator with the young Prince of Hesse-Darmstadt, who, albeit very much in love, was extinguished in the presence of the great Frederick and very near feeling himself honored in being permitted to oblige him by relinquishing his betrothed to the mighty Tzarevitch. The Princess also was very much in love with the Prince of Hesse-Darmstadt, but who could long hesitate between the little duodecimo throne of Hesse-Darmstadt and the colossus throne of Russia? Bridegroom and bride therefore separated with the best understanding, and Frederick the Great could notify his brother that all was satisfactorily arranged. He at once invited the Grand Duke to Berlin to make the personal acquaintance of the Princess, and he and Prince Henry set out together for Germany.

Before their departure Catharine wrote with her own hand the following letter to Prince Henry:

"I take the liberty to transmit to Your Royal Highness the four letters to be delivered by you according to our agreement. One of them is to the King, your brother, and the others are to the Princes and Princesses of Württemberg. I venture to ask Your Royal Highness that as soon as my son shall have, as I hope, declared in favor of the Princess Sophia Dorothea, you will deliver them to their addresses and support them with the persuasive eloquence with which Heaven has so richly endowed Your Royal Highness. The convincing and repeated proofs of friendship for myself which Your Royal Highness has given, your virtues which I so highly prize, and my unbounded confidence in Your Royal Highness, do not allow me to doubt of the successful progress of an affair which I have so much at heart. Could I entrust it to better hands? Your Royal Highness is a negotiator *comme il faut*. You will pardon the expression. I believe there is no other example of an affair of this sort being managed as this will have been. It is the work of the most heartfelt friendship and the most entire confidence. This Princess will be the pledge of it. I shall never see her without being reminded how this affair between the royal house of Prussia and the imperial house of Russia was conducted and effectuated. May it serve to render the tie which unites us indissoluble. I conclude by again thanking Your Royal Highness from my heart for all your trouble and solicitude in this affair, and by begging you to be assured that my gratitude, friendship and esteem, and the regard which I entertain for Your Royal Highness will end only with my life. Zarskoje-Selo, 11th June 1776.—Catharine."

In Berlin the Grand Duke was received with the most distinguished honors. He was introduced at once into the royal palace, where the King stood waiting to receive him at the door of his chamber. Prince Henry presented the Tzarevitch, who addressed the King in these words: "Your Majesty, the causes which have brought me from the extreme north to these happy regions are, the desire which I feel to strengthen the existing friendship between Russia and Prussia perpetually, and my wish to see the Princess who is destined to ascend the imperial throne. This Princess I wish to receive from Your Majesty's hands, and I venture to declare that she will thus be only the more dear to me and to the nation over which she is to reign. Lastly, I have to-day accomplished an object which I have long desired.

I see face to face the greatest ruler in Europe, the object of admiration to our epoch, and the object of wonder to posterity."

The King answered:

"Prince, I do not deserve such praise. You see in me an old and already feeble man. But be assured that I feel myself very happy in seeing within these walls the worthy heir of a mighty Empire, the only son of my best friend, the Great Catharine."

The stream of flattery flowed on. It is worthy of remark that at that very time Frederick the Great was permitting the circulation in Berlin of a satire composed by himself which wittily exposed the little weaknesses of his "best friend, the Great Catharine."

From the King the Grand Duke went to the Queen, where the court were assembled. Here he found the Princess of Württemberg. He was pleased with her, and the contract was concluded. The betrothal took place immediately after, and when the Grand Duke returned to St. Petersburg he was followed by the Princess Sophia Dorothea. Arrived in Russia she united with the Greek Church, receiving the name of Maria Feodorovna, and in the same year her marriage with Paul was solemnized.

In the latter years of Catharine's life the

breach between mother and son widened to such an extent that the Empress made up her mind to dethrone Paul in favor of his eldest son Alexander. Her death prevented the execution of this project and permitted Paul after long years of waiting at last to ascend the throne of the Romanoffs—we dare not say the throne of his fathers.*

The first acts of his reign, as with Peter III., were acts of grace and benignity. He loaded his long neglected family with favors and his subjects with benevolence; he even showed mercy to the favorites of his hated mother, and permitted the old ministers to preserve their

---

* See the works referred to on Catharine II. and Alexander I. Also: Paul. Von einem unbefangenen Beobachter, Leipsig, 1801. Bulau, Geheime Geschichten, 1863, 57-95. Dohm. Denkwürdigkeiten, Hannover, 1815. Achatz von der Asseburgs Denkwürdigkeiten, Berlin, 1842. Bienemann, Aus den Tagen Kaiser Pauls, Leipsig, 1886. Tettenborn, Leben Pauls, Franckfurt, 1804. Paul der Erste, 1802. Notizie sulla morte di Paolo. Kobeko, The Tzarevitch Paul, St. Petersburg, 1882. The Emperor Paul's correspondence with Miss Nelidoff. Russkaja Starina, 1873, 4. Interesting and Remarkable Acts and Anecdotes of the Emperor Paul Petrovitch, Russian Archives, 1864. Memoirs of Semen Poroschin, St. Petersburg, 1844. Afanafsjef, Archives of Juridical and Practical Communications, 1860, 2. Semensky in the Russian Westnik, 1866, 8. Russian Archives, 1867, 2, and 1869, 1.

places. His magnanimity astonished every one.

Soon, however, all this changed, and the effects of his servile education began to betray themselves. The sudden freedom caused him to lose his senses, disordered and bewildered him, drove him mad.

This showed itself first in ways that were harmless—in giving his whole attention to such questions as the shape of hats, the height of grenadier's caps, the color of feathers—to boots, cockades, and sword belts. Any one appearing before him with brightly polished buttons and who hastened to don the new uniform which he had prescribed was loaded with orders and honors, while any persons who presumed to exhibit themselves in the old uniform fared badly. Atrocious misdemeanors of this nature were punished by degradation from the rank of general to that of a private soldier, even with banishment. Foreigners, even, were not spared. The Prussian Ambassador, Tauenzien, who made his appearance at court in a uniform which offended Paul's taste was required to leave St. Petersburg. One day an order was issued forbidding the wearing of round hats, and any one seen with a round hat was struck down by the police or soldiery. Another ukase forbade horses to be harnessed to vehicles after the Russian fashion, and he who disobeyed this order had his carriage stopped by the police and the traces cut.

By an old custom all persons were required upon meeting the Tzar to fall upon their knees, even in a dirty street. Catharine abolished this custom, but Paul revived it with increased rigor. Merchants were prohibited from describing their places of business as "magazines," they must call them "lawkas," "for only the Emperor can have a magazine," said Paul, "a merchant has a shop."

And as in the State so it was with the Emperor's family. If it had given him little concern before ascending the throne, it now gave him still less. The Tzarina Maria Feodorovna was an excellent woman, gentle, mild and modest, and the goodness of her character could not be destroyed by the harsh treatment which she received at the hands of Paul. If Paul might be compared with Peter III., the Empress was not in the least like Catharine. She was a really good wife * and an excellent

---

* Mirabeau in his private correspondence has attempted to cast suspicion upon Maria Feodorovna's conjugal fidelity. He speaks of an adventure of hers with a young nobleman in the French service and of his

mother. Her days were passed in deeds of benevolence and the duties appropriate to her sex and her high position. During Catharine's lifetime she was deprived of her children, but as Empress she was able in a surprisingly short time to obtain a great influence over the characters and opinions of both her sons and daughters. She was reputed to be the busiest woman in the Empire. Besides her household duties and the exacting requirements of her position, she cultivated the fine arts which she really loved. Music, painting, copper-plate engraving, and embroidery, had in her an accomplished pupil.

That she was beautiful we know, but in her bearing there was more of majesty than grace, and she possessed also more heart than cunning. For this reason she, the noblest woman in Russia, was compelled to yield her place to an ugly mistress. Paul, looking about him for a mistress from whom he might derive the pleasure that through his own fault he did not find in his marriage, cast his eyes upon a woman of the name of Nelidoff, whom he brought

---

proposition to the French Government in the event of Catharine's death to avail itself of the services of this man. (Mirabeau, Historie Sécrète de la Cour de Berlin, 1789, I, 96.) The whole story is a pure invention.

into the palace as the companion of the Empress.

Miss Nelidoff was an ugly little woman. Thus in his amours also Paul the Madman resembled Peter the Foolish, who preferred an ugly mistress to a beautiful wife. But Miss Nelidoff was superior to Miss Worenzoff in intellect and manners, and Paul might at least converse with her upon serious subjects. She also endeavored to use her influence for worthy ends, and many good deeds are related of her.

Besides Nelidoff and another mistress whom he had later, Paul had only one favorite, the infamous Kutaisow.

Ivan Kutaisow was by birth a Turk. He was a boy in the Turkish army in 1770, was made prisoner at the capture of Bender and sent to the Grand Duke Paul as a sort of curiosity. Paul converted the young Mohommedan to the Greek faith and retained him in his service, having him instructed in a little French and giving him a superficial education. Kutaisow understood how to make himself useful to the Grand Duke and soon became his trusted confidant. He was the negotiator of Paul's amour with Miss Nelidoff.

When Catharine died and Paul ascended the long wished for throne, the chamber lackey attained a degree of power fitted to excite surprise even in that epoch of rampant favoritism. Kutaisow was the one person who understood the art of managing Paul; he endured all the Tzar's caprices and submitted with patience to blows and outrages. Soon Paul could not exist, could not reign, without Kutaisow. The Emperor's lackey was in reality the ruler of Russia, for whose favor even Besborodko and Pahlen, the official prime ministers, must sue.*

Even Kutaisow was sometimes made to suffer from Paul's caprices, and the most absurd trifle had well-nigh caused the downfall of the favorite. On the occasion of the Tzar's coronation, Kutaisow, whose greed of titles and orders was insatiable, asked for the Order of Anna, second class. Paul, who allowed nothing to be prescribed to him, flew into a rage at this presumption out of all proportion to the offence, beat his favorite and dismissed him from his service. It required the united efforts of the Empress and Miss Nelidoff to appease his anger and prevail upon him to pardon and reinstate Kutaisow. Kutaisow threw himself at

---

*This favorite had again a mistress by the name of Chevalier by whom he was completely ruled and who publicly dispensed titles, offices and estates.

their feet and vowed eternal gratitude. How he kept his vow we shall see hereafter.

Strange to tell the Empress was not jealous of Miss Nelidoff but lived on excellent terms with her, and soon the two arrived at so good an understanding that Miss Nelidoff used all her efforts to prevail upon the Tzar to accede to the wishes of the Empress. Kutaisow remarked this, and began to be uneasy. He made up his mind to accomplish the ruin of them both and to rule as Potemkin had done by means of another amour of which he would be the author.

Upon the occasion of a visit to Moscow, Paul was through the efforts of Kutaisow accorded a magnificent reception. The Tzar observed with much satisfaction to his favorite:

"The people of Moscow love me better than the people of St. Petersburg, for it seems to me that there I am more feared than loved."

"There is nothing surprising in that," answered Kutaisow.

"Why?" asked Paul.

"I dare not express myself more plainly."

"I command you to do so."

"Will Your Majesty engage not to repeat what I say to Miss Nelidoff or the Empress?"

"I promise."

"The cause, then, is this. In Moscow they see you as you really are—good, magnanimous and loving. But in St. Petersburg, if you grant a favor it is always the Empress or Miss Nelidoff who prompted it. For a good act they get all the praise, but when you are severe and punish, the hatred is all yours."

"Yes, you are right, and this must not continue. They say also that I am ruled by my wife and Nelidoff?"

"Not exactly ruled—but, yes, Your Majesty, I cannot longer refrain from telling you—I must say it, whatever it may cost me, they say that you allow yourself to be governed by these two ladies."

"Ah! my dears," began Paul furiously, "I will let you see whether I am ruled by you or not."

And he rushed to a table and began to write. But Kutaisow, for whom the affair was travelling too fast, conjured him not to act hastily.

The next day at a court ball which Paul attended, he saw Kutaisow's creature, the beautiful sixteen-years-old Lopuchin. Notwithstanding her youth she was well advanced in the arts of coquetry. She placed herself always in a position where she would attract the Tzar's attention, followed him wherever he went, and in whatever direction he turned his eyes he saw hers fixed upon him as if in ecstasy. He said to an attendant, who was also a creature of Kutaisow's:

"Why does that beautiful girl yonder follow me wherever I go?"

"She has fallen in love with Your Majesty. Since she has seen you she has lost her senses."

The Emperor smiled with satisfaction and said:

"But she is so young—a mere child."

"Oh, she is sixteen," was the answer.

"H—m, really this is not so bad," said the Tzar, becoming more observant and moving closer to her.

He spoke to her, conversed with her awhile, found her artless and amusing, made up his mind to take compassion on the infatuated damsel, and calling Kutaisow commissioned him to arrange the affair with the girl's father.

This was quickly done and Paul had his new mistress.

When the Emperor returned to St. Petersburg he gave an order for the removal of Lopuchin, the girl's father, to St. Petersburg.

The Empress and Miss Nelidoff soon began to feel the effect of the change. One day Paul abused so badly the Vice-Chancellor, Prince Kurakin, a dependent of the Empress, that he fell ill, and upon the Empress attempting to interpose in Kurakin's behalf the Tzar's rage fell upon herself. She discerned whence arose the trouble, and being informed that both Lopuchin and his daughter were about to remove to St. Petersburg she wrote a threatening letter to the girl designed to deter her from carrying out her intentions. The letter was communicated to Paul and threw him into the most violent rage. He fell upon the Empress and Nelidoff like a wild beast and abused them unmercifully. Miss Nelidoff requested to be permitted to retire from the court. The Emperor was quite willing, but out of perverseness he refused. The rejected mistress fled without his permission and retired to her estate.

Anna Petrovna Lopuchina understood better than Nelidoff had done how to turn her position to advantage. In her father's name she requested from the Tzar the rank of countess, as was suitable, she said, for the Emperor's mistress.

"You are right," said Paul, "you wish to be a countess? I make you a princess."

And the next day, Peter Lopuchin was made a prince. Paul now imitated Peter the Third in maltreating every one who was friendly to his wife. The most insignificant occasion furnished him with the pretext. It was enough to have been seen speaking two or three times with the Empress to incur his displeasure. Count Vielhorsky, who as her steward had frequent occasion to communicate with her, approached her at a court ball requesting some instructions. Paul remarking it, observed to the Grand Duke Alexander, indicating the Count:

"There is no occasion for him to bring his wash here."

The Grand Duke made a sign to the Count to withdraw. Count Vielhorsky quitted the Empress and moved toward a table where the game of Boston was being played. He had no sooner joined the players than Paul said to the Grand Duke:

"See how he keeps within ear-shot, that he may overhear what we are saying. He is insolent."

The Grand Duke again signed to the Count, but the sign was not remarked. Paul then called out:

"Listen, Count, do you know that von Naryschkin is the Empress's steward?"

The occasion of a quarrel with Count Stroganoff was if possible still more insignificant. This was brought about by the Count's taking the side of the Empress in a question of the weather.

The Emperor being at Paulowsk, proposed to the Empress a walk. With a glance toward the window the latter said :

"I fear it is going to rain."

"What do you say?" asked Paul of Count Stroganoff who happened to be present.

The Count looked out and answered :

"It is very cloudy ; we may therefore expect before very long to have rain."

"Aha!" exclaimed Paul. "You agree with the Empress solely for the purpose of vexing me. I am tired of all this falseness. It seems to me, Count, that we do not any longer suit each other. You never understand me. Moreover you are wanted at St. Petersburg, and I advise you to return there at once. This time I hope you understand me."

Count Stroganoff made a profound bow to the demented monarch and withdrew.

Paul often placed his wife on an elevated point that she might serve his troops as a picket. There stood the poor, patient woman for hours in snow or rain, heat or cold, in a position truly worthy of an Empress !

So Paul like Peter the Third made himself hated by his family and hated and despised by his people and the principal men of the Empire until at last the determination ripened among them to rid themselves of the tyrant. He was so fearful of a violent death that he caused a palace to be built constructed with a view to ensuring his safety, and of which he took possession while the walls were still wet. The Empress fell ill, and also the Grand Duke Alexander. Only Paul felt himself well in this fortified tower, protected by moats, drawbridges and secret corridors which seemed to make it impenetrable for any stranger.

Nevertheless this palace became the Tzar's tomb. In spite of all his measures of precaution the avengers of the people's wrongs found their way to the Emperor and strangled him, after he had during five years tormented the country and his family.

Even his most faithful and loyal followers—alas! they were few—could not deny that never had a change of rulers been received with a more lively satisfaction.

To Paul the Eccentric succeeded Alexander the Good—the Blessed.

THE DESCENDANTS OF PAUL THE ECCENTRIC.

The Grand Duchess Alexandra and Gustavus IV. of Sweden.—Constantine Paulovitch and His Worthy Son.—Alexander the Blessed.—Madam Krüdener.—Nicholas the Virtuous and His Amours.—Alexander II. and the Princess Dolgorucky.

A FAVORITE scheme of Catharine II. was the marriage of her granddaughter, the Grand Duchess Alexandra to the Crown Prince of Sweden, afterwards Gustavus IV. Alexandra grew up in the anticipation of one day wearing the crown of Sweden, and all about her talked in a manner fitted to foster the expectation and addressed her jestingly as the "little Queen." While she was quite a child the Empress one day showed her a portfolio containing the portraits of several young princes, and said to the little Grand Duchess: "See here, child, which of these would you like for your husband?"

"This one," immediately answered Alexandra, pointing to the Crown Prince of Sweden, whom already her childish fancy had dwelt on as her husband and who had been held up before her as an ideal person.

Catharine was delighted, fancying that this answer betrayed a predisposition of the child's heart for her predestined husband, overlooking the circumstance that the pictures were marked with the names of the originals, and that that was the reason why "her heart had spoken for the Prince." She imagined she had heard the voice of destiny, and pursued her project with increased ardor. It was, as may be supposed, political considerations rather than solicitude for the future of her granddaughter that led her to attach such importance to its success. The object of the proposed marriage was nothing less than to unite the crown of Sweden to that of Russia.

After the violent death of Gustavus III. his brother Charles, the Duke of Södermanland, had become regent in the name of the young heir. Duke Charles was not in the least disposed to enter into Catharine's project, and he was not rendered more favorable to it after she had sent assassins to disembarrass her of the reluctant regent.

To destroy forever her hope of a Swedish alliance, he formally betrothed the Crown Prince to the Princess Louisa Charlotte of Mecklenburg-Schwerin, daughter of Duke Frederick Francis. The news of this betrothal was announced by a special messenger to the Court of Russia, but the indignant Catharine showed the Swedish envoy the door, and threatened severely the Duke of Mecklenburg if he did not at once dissolve the contract.

It seemed as if the King of Sweden was to be constrained by force to wed the Grand Duchess.

The latter meanwhile had developed into a beautiful and attractive girl, well worthy of the best of princes. The rumor therefore easily spread that the young King of Sweden was desperately enamoured of the Grand Duchess Alexandra, but was being forced by his uncle's tyranny to marry the Princess of Mecklenburg. Catharine left nothing undone to bring Gustavus himself to this opinion. Officials high and low and all the associates of the young Prince were bribed to pour into his ears the most marvellous tales of the enchanting beauty of the Grand Duchess, and it really seemed as if in the youthful heart of Gustavus the romantic tales breathed into his ear had ended by awakening an interest in her.

For it is not otherwise to be explained that his uncle, the regent, suddenly yielded. The Mecklenburg betrothal was broken off, and the young King, accompanied by the regent, went on a visit to St. Petersburg in order—as Catharine said—that the young people, who were already in love, might become acquainted and if mutually pleased might find their happiness in each other.

Catharine saw her game won. That the Grand Duchess would please the King she did not doubt, and she was prepared to propitiate the regent by paying him the most distinguished attentions.

The young King of Sweden arrived in St. Petersburg with his uncle August 14, 1796, and alighted at the residence of the Ambassador Stedingk. The whole population of the capital streamed through the streets to see the young monarch whose possession had enkindled so warm a contest. The Empress received the King at the " Hermitage " and was delighted with him, " almost in love with him," as she expressed herself to her circle. He offered to kiss her hand, which she refused, whereupon the gallant young monarch said :

"If your Majesty will not allow it as Empres, you will I hope permit me to kiss the hand of the woman for whom I have so much respect and admiration."

The meeting of the prospective bridegroom with the Grand Duchess was interesting. Both were greatly embarrassed, and the fact that all eyes were turned upon them was not fitted to diminish their natural confusion.

They were mutually pleased.

Alexandra, although but fourteen, was in the full bloom of beauty, a flower which appeared all the more brilliant in the midst of this northern semi-civilization. Her bearing was noble and elegant, her face beautiful, and every movement full of grace. Gayety and innocence sat smiling on her brow encircled with blond tresses; candor and purity, goodness and gentleness beamed from her eyes. Gustavus with his sixteen years was as finished a chevalier as a girl could have made the ideal of her dreams. He was tall and slender, intelligent and mature, and in his bearing there was great gentleness and modesty, and withal kingly pride. In spite of his youth he was not shy. His address was free and unconstrained, courteous and insinuating. The splendors which he saw around him seemed not to dazzle him;

only before the brightness of Alexandra's eyes he bowed his head.

All was exultation ; the project of Catharine received universal praise. Even the regent could not refrain from participating in the general satisfaction. It was a festive time for all the city in which even the lowest of the people shared. The young King was welcomed with ovations wherever he showed himself, and the nobles vied with each other in the splendor of the entertainments which they gave in honor of the guest.

Catharine was astonished at the greatness of her success. The King and Grand Duchess were enchanted with each other and could not separate from each other for a moment. The formal betrothal was fixed for the 10th of September, 1796, to be soon followed by the marriage. All was ready and no hindrance now stood in the way.

Yes, one—religion.

Catharine wished, more for the sake of flattering the national pride than out of love for the Greek Church, that the Queen of Sweden should continue in the exercise of the Russian religion. Gustavus was not consulted, he was believed to be sufficiently in love to overlook everything.

The hour of the betrothal arrived. With all the pomp of circumstance the great dignitaries of the Empire assembled in the throne room, Catharine, magnificently attired, seemed to have grown young with joy. At half past seven the Grand Duchess appeared, beamingly expectant of meeting her betrothed.

But he had not come, and he did not.

And the reason why he did not was this:

As the King was preparing for the betrothal the diplomate Markoff arrived and laid before him the marriage contract which he was to sign. The contract contained articles to the effect that the Grand Duchess should not only be permitted to retain her own religion, but that there should be erected for her in the royal palace a special chapel with its attendant priests, and to this stipulation were added several very dubious obligations which as a result of the marriage Sweden would contract toward Russia.

The King was not a little astonished. Such pretensions had long since ceased to be urged. He answered: "It is impossible. I will not, for the love I bear the Grand Duchess, seek to lay any restraint upon her conscience and she may, if it so please her, continue to practice her own religion, but it does not comport with my position to consent to the establishment in the palace of a chapel for her use with appropriate ministrations. She should not, so far as public ceremonies are concerned, show herself contrary to the religion of the country."

The Russian minister was startled and embarrassed. At a loss how to reply he hurried off 'to take counsel of Suboff, who then held sway. Suboff dared not report the matter to the Empress, so he hastened to the King and entreated him to yield for the present, and all would be satisfactorily arranged. The regent also exerted his influence, but the intractable young monarch only answered:

"No and no. I will not, I cannot; I will sign nothing of the sort." As they continued to storm him he withdrew angrily to his chamber and locked himself in.

The Empress, who was not easily disconcerted, this time was confounded. The great, the powerful Catharine to be thus thwarted by a young King of Sweden! It was unheard of! It was necessary to dismiss the court and the assembled guests, to dismantle the splendidly decorated throne room and to extinguish the hundred torches lighted in honor of Hymen.

But the saddest sacrifice of the catastrophe

was the unfortunate Grand Duchess, who fell ill in consequence.

The second day after the occurrence of this scandal was the birthday of the Grand Duchess Anna Feodorovna, before her marriage the Princess Julie Henriette of Saxe-Coburg, the unhappy wife of the Grand Duke Constantine. According to court etiquette a ball had to be held in honor of the day, but never was court ball so gloomy. The King of Sweden was present but Catharine did not address a word to him, and every one was awkward and embarrassed. The Grand Duchess Alexandra was confined to her bed and did not appear. The King danced with some of the Princesses, said a few words to the Grand Duke Alexander, and departed, never again to visit the Russian court. A few days after, he quitted the country leaving Catharine to her wrath and the innocent Alexandra to her grief.

Gustavus and Alexandra both married, and both were unfortunate. The Grand Duchess married Joseph, hereditary Prince of Hungary, and died at Buda on the 4th of March, 1801, not having reached the age of eighteen.

Gustavus IV. married on October 3, 1797, the Princess Frederica of Baden, sister-in-law of the Grand Duke Alexander, but his marriage was unhappy. After his dethronement in 1809 he separated from his family and his wife and lived at Basle under the name of Colonel Gustavson in great poverty and distress until his death, which took place in February, 1837, at St. Galle. He died alone and neglected.

Paul had by Maria Feodorovna ten children, eight of whom survived him.

The works on Catharine and Paul.—Memoirs of Martikoff in the " Ssara," 1871; Comtesse Choiseul Gouffier, Mémoires Historiques sur l'Empereur Alexandre I.,Paris, 1829; La Harpe, Von Suchomlinof, St. Petersburg, 1871; Pypin, the Emperor Alexander and the Quakers; In the Westnik Jewropy, 1869, 10; Pypin, Madam Krüdener, Westnik Jewropy, 1869, 8 and 9; Pypin, Social Movements Under Alexander I., 1871; Baronesse de Stael, Dix Années d'Exile, 1818-1821; Schnitzler, Histoire in time de la Russie, Paris, 1826; Rabbe, Histoire d'Alexandre I., Paris, 1826; La Garde, Reise von Moskau nach Wein über Konstantinopel, Heidelberg, 1825; Comtesse Choiseul Gouffier, Reminiscences sur l'Empereur Alexandre I., Besancon, 1862; Bogdanovitch, History of the Reign of Alexander the First, St. Petersburg, 1869, 4 vol.; Golowin, Geschichte Alexanders des Ersten, Leipsig, 1859; Joynville, Life and Times of Alexander I., London, 1875; Dr. Ch. Müller, St. Petersburg, Ein Beitrag zur Geschichte unserer Zeit, Mainz, 1813; L'Hermite en Russie, par Dupré de St. Maure, 1829; Eynard Vie de Mme. de Krüdener, Paris, 1849; Capefigue, La Baronne de Krüdener et l'Empereur Alexander I., Paris, 1866; Frau von Krüdener, Ein Zeitgemalde, Bern, 1868; Lacroix, Mme. de Krüdener, Paris, 1880; Sketches from the Life of

While Catharine lived, Paul and Maria were scarcely permitted to have anything to do with their children. Even in regard to the marriage of their daughter to the King of Sweden they were not consulted, and the King during the six weeks which he spent in St. Petersburg did not once visit the parents of his prospective bride. Of the marriage of the Grand Duke Alexander we will speak hereafter.

The Grand Duke Constantine married the Princess Julie Henriette of Saxe-Coburg, who thus was condemned to an unspeakably unhappy existence until the luckless marriage was dissolved by a separation. Constantine afterwards led the most profligate life imaginable until, weary of excesses, he determined upon a second marriage. On the 24th pay of May, 1820, he married the Polish Countess, Johanna Antonovna Grundzynska, whom Alexander I. made Princess of Lowicz. On account of this unequal marriage Constantine renounced the succession—Alexander having no children—in favor of his brother Nicholas.

Constantine, "the terror of Poland," died on

Nicholas I., Graz, 1878; Golovine, La Russie sous Nicholas, Paris, 1845; Lacroix, Mystéres de la Russie, Paris, 1845; Gagern, Nicolaus I.; Crusenstolpe, Der Russiche Hof, Hamburg, 1855; Laferte, Alexander II. Génève 1882.

the 27th of June 1831 of cholera; his wife on the 29th of November of the same year.

The example of Constantine's morals was followed by his son Nicholas Constantinovitch. The mistress of Nicholas, the daughter of an American clergyman named Blackwood, visited him in the Winter Palace. When this came to the knowledge of his father, he summoned his son, and said to him: "You are aware that it is forbidden to receive women in the Palace. Why have you done so?"

"My father is not himself so scrupulous."

The father gave his impertinent son a blow, which was promptly returned to him.

At the same time with this occurrence, it came to light that the Grand Duke Nicholas Constantinovitch had stolen his mother's jewels and valuable pictures of saints, and sold or presented them to his American mistress.

What was to be done with him?

It was decided to pronounce him insane and send him to Bessarabia.

Miss Blackwood prepared her stocking betimes and conveyed the jewels and pictures in safety to Paris and London. She offered the letters of her former lover to the Russian Ambassador for a half million francs, but failing to realize a sou for them worked up the letters and her piquant experiences under the name of "Letters of an American," which were published in Paris. Later, having squandered everything she possessed, she robbed an Englishman at Nice and ended in a house of correction.

When the time arrived to choose a wife for the Grand Duke Alexander, Paul's oldest son, Catharine invited to St. Petersburg the two Princesses of Baden-Durlach, whose aunt Wilhelmine had been the first wife of Paul. At the end of the autumn of 1792 they arrived at the Russian court and were received by Catharine in the palace of the late Potemkin. They fell at her feet and wept, kissed her dress and hands, for on the progress from their German home to the Russian capital the young inexperienced creatures, who were accompanied only by Russian officials, had undergone much. Catharine consoled and encouraged them, made them presents of jewels and stuffs, and the Band of the Order of Catharine.

The next day the princesses made the acquaintance of the Grand Duke, then fifteen years old, who found the elder of them quite pretty. His brother Constantine, two years younger than himself, who already as a boy gave evidence that he was not distinguished for gallantry, or nobility of character, remarked:

"I see nothing to admire in either. They ought to be sent to Mittau to Prince Biron of Courland. They are good enough for him."

Catharine, on hearing Alexander's judgment, decided in favor of the elder princess. The other was sent home and married afterwards Gustavus of Sweden.

Alexander and Louise were much pleased with each other. She accepted the Greek religion and received the name of Elizabeth Alexejewna. In May, 1793, the final betrothal was celebrated with great pomp. Catharine had brought three wars to a successful issue, and the celebration of her triumph lent additional brilliancy to the festivities. Conqured Swedes and Poles, Khans of Tartary, Ambassadors from Turkish Pashas, Envoys from Moldavia and Greece, vied with each other in doing homage to the great Empress.

On the 9th of October, 1793, the marriage was celebrated. The fairest hopes were built upon the young Prince and his consort. Masson de Blamont, a contemporary author of "Secret Memoirs of Russia," has given an enthusiastic description of the young Grand Duke, whom he speaks of as the almost realized ideal which delights us in Telemachus, who, though far from possessing a Ulysses for his father or a Mentor for his preceptor, had a mother who was possessed of all the domestic virtues of Penelope. The same faults also might be attributed to him as those with which Fenelon reproached his idealized pupil, but they should rather be characterized as deficiencies arising out of a lack of qualities which had either not been developed in him or had been smothered by the wretched atmosphere in which he lived. He had sublime ideas, a constant disposition, a correct judgment, shrewd intelligence and rare prudence, joined to a caution and reserve which did not belong to his age and which would have been falseness had they not been accounted for by the constrained position in which he found himself between his father and grandmother. He was naturally open-hearted and free from deceit.

From his mother he had his height and his beauty, his gentleness, and disposition to do good. In no external traits did he bear any resemblance to his father, whom he had more reason to fear than to love as he was himself more feared than loved by Paul. For it was no secret to him that Catharine entertained a project of supplanting him in favor of his son.

During Paul's short reign all eyes turned

with longing toward Alexander. The army worshipped him, statesmen admired his understanding, the people, the unhappy people, shouted with joy whenever he appeared. When Paul came to his end Alexander succeeded to the throne amid universal joy. It was the dawning of a day of peace and happiness, such happiness that already during his lifetime they gave him the name of "the Blessed."

Reform followed reform. The secret tribunal was abolished, Paul's torture-chambers disappeared, the emancipation of the serfs was begun. The censure became more lax, books and newspapers might circulate freely, the expenses of the court were diminished, taxes were reduced the army decreased. Peace! Peace! Peace! was the watchword of the Blessed peace Emperor!

But he was an Emperor in Russia. There monarchs, even liberal ones, have not for a long time been of use, and perhaps—who knows?—will not much longer be in use.

Russia wants a ruler like Nicholas rather than gentle, yielding natures like Alexander I. and II.

And Alexander I., the Good, the Gentle, the Blessed, was very yielding, very weak. He lacked boldness and self-confidence, and it was easy for mischievous persons to insinuate themselves into his favor. At the last he fell completely under the influence of a baleful pietism. And strange! it was a Protestant woman who wove about him the meshes of mysticism that effected his ruin.

During his whole reign Alexander had been haunted by terrible recollections of the murder of Paul, which tempted to the belief that the son had participated in it. He sought refuge at last from these tormenting memories in the mysteries of religion, and all his ideals grew pale, all his earthly desires were swallowed up in them, his good intentions toward the country were forgotten. A religious fanatic, the Baroness Krüdener, who after a youth of sin had thrown herself into the arms of religion and had become a prophetess, obtained a degree of influence over her contemporaries, even the best and greatest, which is to-day incomprehensible. The Emperor fell completely under her spell and became a zealous adherent of this "prophetess" and visionary. Everything was deferred to religion, even the most weighty affairs of state were determined by it.

"At the conference with my ministers it often happened that they did not share my principles, that some entirely dissented therefrom. In such cases, without entering into any discussion I have turned to God with earnest prayer, and generally He has helped me and has converted my ministers to those principles of gentleness and justice which I had upheld."

While Alexander was thus abandoning himself to pietism, the conduct of affairs of state was left in the hands of favorites, especially in those of General Araktsschajeff, a man of an extremely peaceful temper, it is true, but dishonest, capricious and unenlightened. And the worst of all was that this same Araktsschajeff was not even independent, but was a marionette in the hands of numerous mistresses before whom the most exalted in the land sought to efface themselves.

All the bright promises with which the reign of Alexander had begun were blasted, the hopes of a freer existence in the Empire of the Tzars sank and disappeared amid the rottenness and corruption of official life, the ineradicable misery. The censure, which in the early part of the reign of Alexander the Blessed had been relaxed, was again rigidly enforced, books, even innocent ones from foreign countries, were prohibited, excessive restrictions were placed upon the freedom of education, and freemasonry, which had been tolerated, was suppressed throughout the Empire. And as with his relations with the state so with the Emperor's family relations. His marriage had seemed at first extremely happy. The young wife of the Grand Duke was beautiful, tall and distinguished in appearance, pure and refined, full of intellect and talent, taste and feeling.

The Comte de la Gardie, at the date of the Congress of Vienna, found her still charming. "She has a charming face, and eyes which mirror the purity of her soul. She has the prettiest light blond hair, which she usually wears falling over her shoulders; her step is so singularly graceful that it is not easy for her to disguise herself by a mask. *Incessu patuit Dea.* In her a bright mind is united with a noble character, a love of the fine arts and an inexhaustible benevolence.

Benevolence! This was her most beautiful virtue. Her good deeds were done in silence, where and as the occasion offered. She carried consolation and joy into the huts of the poor and into the palaces of the rich, where often consolation is most needed.

Yet she was herself the most unhappy woman in Russia. Her domestic life was blighted by the want of children. Two daughters born in the first years of her marriage had died in tender infancy, and destiny had made her no amends. The noble Princess lacked the sensuality and coquetry which might, notwithstanding, have attached her husband to her, and he sought elsewhere the joys of love which he believed he could not find in his home.

Alexander had many mistresses, but one in particular was able to bind him to her for eleven years. She was the wife of another, and her relations with the Tzar, therefore, were a double crime. Three children were born to them, two of whom died in infancy. The surviving child was a daughter named Sophia— a beautiful girl who made the secret happiness of the Tzar's life. But her health failed while still in the bloom of youth, as if in expiation of the sins of her parents. Alexander employed every means for her recovery and, hoping to the last, joyfully consented to her marriage with a worthy young man of a burgher family. Beautiful ornaments were ordered from Paris to deck the bride, but when they arrived the beautiful betrothed lay on her bier.

Alexander was crushed. He felt the wrath of Heaven upon him. When his neglected wife on learning the death of Sophia wrote him words of tenderest sympathy he felt the injustice he had done her and turned, repentant, to the heart of his Elizabeth. An ardent affection sprung up between them, but their happiness was short-lived. The griefs which they had passed through had undermined the health of both, and they died toward the end of 1825 within a short period of each other.

Nicholas, the brother and successor of Alexander and ten years his junior, received from some of his contemporaries the name of "the Austere." Yet his austerity consisted only in certain external observances. To his wife Alexandra, the daughter of Queen Louisa, he was careful to testify in public the utmost regard and consideration. Of the character of the latter differing judgments have been formed by contemporaries and historians. It is certain that she was vain and pleasure-loving, and if beautiful in her youth, she early became faded and ugly. Nevertheless, Nicholas was scrupulously affectionate and attentive, addressed her as "little mother" and when at Naples she became ill, he carried her upstairs in his arms.

All this was a matter of external decorum. He forbade young girls to attend theatres when indecent plays were performed, tolerated no adventures of gallantry at the court, and punished with severity breaches of the marriage vow, yet he permitted himself everything, and in immorality was behind none of his predecessors on the throne of the Tzars. Prince Dologorucky was his "Fisher," and furnished him his opportunities. Furthermore, this same Emperor who punished so severely breaches of conjugal faith had a special preference for married women. Of the great number of his mistresses I will mention only a few.

One was a Madam von Stolypin, niece of Prince Ssergey Trubetskoy. Her husband died broken-hearted and his bereaved widow married Prince Woronzoff.

A Miss Nelidoff, a relative of Paul's mistress of that name played a considerable rôle in the life of Nicholas. Count Kleinmichel was the go-between and protector of this liaison. The meetings of the lovers took place at his house and the Countess Kleinmichel had to feign pregnancy when Miss Nelidoff became so in reality by the Tzar. All the children born of this connection passed for the children of the Count and Countess Kleinmichel.

Miss Nelidoff, like her relative of the same name, did not lack noble qualities. When Nicholas died and she came into possession of some millions which he had bequeathed to her she at once presented the whole bequest to the soldiers wounded at Sebastopol. And she was not very rich, for Nicholas was aways a curmudgeon.

His son and heir, the Tzar-Emancipator lavished all the more. Alexander II. was good and noble, but mediocre and weak, often a mere tool in the hands of his mistresses. His life closed in the midst of a romantic idyl, his relations with the Princess Dolgorucky, whom he called Yurevsky and whom he married with the left hand. Death came in 1881 to break up this happy connection. The Empress widow went to Italy, where she lived a quiet and retired life on the rental of the eighty millions which had been left her by Alexander. Her oldest son George was graciously received by his half-brother Alexander III. and became a lieutenant in the fleet at Kronstadt.

THE END.